Problems *with* Atonement

The Origins of, and Controversy about, the Atonement Doctrine

Stephen Finlan

A Michael Glazier Book

LITURGICAL PRESS
Collegeville, Minnesota

www.litpress.org

A Michael Glazier Book published by the Liturgical Press

Cover design by David Manahan, O.S.B. Illustration: *The Crucifixion* by Georges Rouault, courtesy of The Minneapolis Institute of Arts.

Library of Congress Cataloging-in-Publication Data

Finlan, Stephen.
    Problems with atonement : the origins of, and controversy about, the atonement doctrine / Stephen Finlan.
        p. cm.
    Summary: "Examines the origins and outcomes of the Christian doctrine of atonement : its biblical foundations, development, and theological questions surrounding it, including questions about its relationship to the Incarnation" — Provided by publisher.
    "A Michael Glazier book."
    Includes bibliographical references and index.
    ISBN-13: 978-0-8146-5220-6 (pbk. : alk. paper)
    ISBN-10: 0-8146-5220-4 (pbk. : alk. paper)
    1. Atonement—History of doctrines. I. Title.

BT263.F56 2005
232'.3—dc22   2005003128

Contents

Abbreviations

AB—Anchor Bible

ABD—Anchor Bible Dictionary

ANE—Ancient Near East

ANRW—Aufstieg und Niedergang der Römischen Welt

ATR—Anglican Theological Review

BAGD—A Greek-English Lexicon of the New Testament and Other Early Christian Literature, by Walter Bauer. Translated and adapted by William F. Arndt and F. Wilbur Gingrich. Second edition. Chicago: University of Chicago Press, 1979.

B.C.E.—Before Common Era

BJS—Brown Judaic Studies

CBQ—Catholic Biblical Quarterly

C.E.—Common Era

CTQ—Concordia Theological Quarterly

ETL—Ephemerides theologicae lovanienses

ExpT—Expository Times

HB—Hebrew Bible

HDR—Harvard Dissertations in Religion

ICC—International Critical Commentary

idem—"by the same author"

JAOS—Journal of the American Oriental Society

JBL—Journal of Biblical Literature

JSJ—Journal for the Study of Judaism

JSJ Sup—*Journal for the Study of Judaism,* Supplement Series

JSNT—Journal for the Study of the New Testament

JSNT Sup—*Journal for the Study of the New Testament*, Supplement Series

JSOT Sup—*Journal for the Study of the Old Testament*, Supplement Series

JTS—*Journal of Theological Studies*

LXX—the Septuagint, the Greek translation of the OT

MT—Masoretic Text

n.s.—new series

NAB—New American Bible

NASB—New American Standard Bible

NovTSup—*Novum Testamentum*, Supplement Series

NT—New Testament

NTS—*New Testament Studies*

OT—Old Testament

PRSt—*Perspectives in Religious Studies*

SBLDS—Society of Biblical Literature Dissertation Series

SBLSBS—Society of Biblical Literature Sources for Biblical Study

SBLSP—*Society of Biblical Literature Seminar Papers*

SBT—Studies in Biblical Theology

SJLA—Studies in Judaism in Late Antiquity

SJT—*Scottish Journal of Theology*

SNTSMS—Society for New Testament Studies Monograph Series

TDNT—*Theological Dictionary of the New Testament*

WBC—Word Biblical Commentary

WMANT—Wissenschaftliche Monographien zum Alten und Neuen Testament

WUNT—Wissenschaftliche Untersuchungen zum Neuen Testament

ZAW—*Zeitschrift für die Alttestamentliche Wissenschaft*

Standards

Except where indicated, NRSV is the translation of the Bible used throughout. With German authors, if there is a published English translation, that has been used. If no English is available, the translation is my own, and the title in the footnote remains in German.

Introduction

W hy "problems"? What is most noticeable about the literature on atonement written in the last 150 years is the intense concern with *problems* that the authors (and presumably the readers) have with the traditional doctrines of atonement. The agenda is largely set by the widespread dismay regarding the received doctrines of atonement, for instance, such notions as these:

- God's honor was damaged by human sin;
- God demanded a bloody victim—innocent or guilty—to pay for human sin;
- God was persuaded to alter God's verdict against humanity when the Son of God offered to endure humanity's punishment;
- the death of the Son thus functioned as a payoff; salvation was purchased.

Most strategies for dealing with objections to these doctrines involve separating the objectionable from the biblical, either showing that the objectionable doctrines do not occur in the Bible, or that they do occur but are not objectionable when properly explained. An example of these options is seen in two approaches to the suggestion that God was somehow persuaded or bought-off. Moule says this is "a pernicious travesty of the gospel";[1] the event was not "a sacrifice offered to God," but God's own expenditure and (on Jesus' side) "the offering of glad and affirmative obedience."[2]

However, another respected British scholar sees no travesty, but only an ordinary transaction, "parallel to the gift of flowers in human

---

[1] C.F.D. Moule, "Preaching the Atonement," in *Epworth Review* 10, no. 2 (1983) 70. R. J. Campbell calls it a "monstrous assertion" that acts "as a kind of anaesthetic to the moral instincts" (*Christianity and the Social Order* [London: Chapman and Hall, 1907] 138).

[2] Moule, "Preaching," 75.

relationships."[3] Flowers, of course, are the standard offering of appeasement in the case of strained domestic relationships. Rather than reject the concept of appeasing God, this author attempts to make appeasement inoffensive.

Another example is seen in two different stances on the doctrine of eternal damnation, that is, eternal torment: Fudge says the doctrine is "unbiblical, unreasonable and unnecessary,"[4] but Martin Luther finds it to be biblical, and all objections to be irrelevant: God does not care if God appears to be arbitrary and unfair to us.[5] Each author purports to defend biblical doctrine. Fudge separates the objectionable from the biblical; Luther finds the same doctrine in the Bible but refuses to allow it to be objectionable, because human wisdom is incompetent to object to anything biblical.

There is a certain problem in using the word "atonement" since ancient atonement ideas were connected with ceremonial cleansings of temple installations, while the English word "atonement" is formed from the agreeable idea of *at-one-ment*: union. In the last hundred years there has been a growth industry in such books as *At Onement: or, Reconciliation with God;*[6] *The Creative Work of Jesus;*[7] *The Sufferings and the Glory;*[8] and *The Glory of the Atonement*[9]—books that emphasize reconciliation and downplay the cultic (sacrifice and scapegoat) background, thus making atonement more palatable.

This book is not like those other books; I will not be offering a new and acceptable doctrine of atonement. I will, instead, notice precisely those aspects of atonement that have troubled the interpreters of the

---

[3] John Goldingay, "Old Testament Sacrifice and the Death of Christ," in *Atonement Today*, ed. John Goldingay (London: SPCK, 1995) 4. It is best seen as "a gift offered to God," not as something that takes place within a structure "of authority, power, business, or law" (6).

[4] Edward William Fudge wrote this portion, in a book he coauthors with Robert A. Peterson, *Two Views of Hell: A Biblical and Theological Dialogue* (Downers Grove, Ill.: IVP, 2000) 193; cf. 41, 207–8.

[5] *Bondage of the Will*, Parts 6 and 19; *Martin Luther: Selections from His Writings*, ed. John Dillenberger (Garden City, N.Y.: Doubleday, 1961) 195–6, 199–201.

[6] By George Coulson Workman (New York: Fleming H. Revell, 1911).

[7] By Daniel Lamont (London: James Clarke & Co., 1924).

[8] By Rendel Harris (London: Headley Brothers, 1915).

[9] *The Glory of the Atonement: Biblical, Historical and Practical Perspectives*, ed. Charles E. Hill, and Frank A. James III (Downers Grove, Ill.: IVP, 2004). The title and some of the argumentation is spiritualizing, but these authors do not downplay the sacrificial transaction; they are quite comfortable with the Calvinist notion that sacrifice involves "the setting aside of God's wrath" (D. A. Carson, "Atonement in Romans 3:21-26," 130).

last 150 years, and draw attention to the pattern of correction, rationalization, and spiritualization that has dominated both scholarly and confessional discourse on atonement.

But, in fairness, I must also notice the fact that such rationalization takes place in all sacrificial traditions. A spiritualizing reinterpretation and metaphorical redefining of sacrifice takes place in all sacrificial cultures, for instance in India, where animal sacrifice has been replaced by rituals that internalize and *represent* sacrifice, and vegetarian priests still recite sacrificial texts. Thus, "problems with atonement" overlap with "problems with sacrifice." The Christian notion of Christ as the final sacrifice who replaces all animal sacrifices, has some interesting parallels in the critique of, and substitution for, violent sacrificial rituals in Greek and Indian cultures, and I will briefly mention some details at appropriate places.

The Incarnation

It is helpful to examine certain key doctrines in Christian thought, and to understand how they relate to each other. Christianity inherits a number of its central doctrines from Judaism: monotheism, Providence, a final judgment. But there is a central doctrine that is unique to Christianity: the Incarnation. Though it borrows features from various places, the doctrine of the Incarnation itself does not descend from any Jewish or Gentile source.

A cluster of important doctrines revolves around the idea of the Incarnation:

- **divinity:** concepts of the divinity of Jesus and his genetic relationship to God;
- **approach:** concepts of how God approaches humanity through the Son, and humanity approaches God through the Son;
- **suffering:** ideas of how God shares in human suffering through the Son's suffering;
- **atonement:** doctrines of the Son's death on the cross as a sacrifice or other ritual action that restores the relationship with God and cleanses away human sin; many Christians' understandings of the kindness of God are inextricably entwined with their notions of a special saving work accomplished by Christ on the cross. For many Christians, the significance of the Incarnation is that it ended in an atoning death, one that cleansed impurity, carried away sin, or purchased salvation.

The Incarnation cannot be interpreted without some concept of the divinity of Christ; otherwise, his taking on earthly flesh is no different from anyone else's living an earth life. Those who teach that every person is as divine as Christ is (such as the Gnostic *Gospel of Philip*), lose sight of the Incarnation, and cannot really be called Christian. Incarnation must entail something about the unique divinity of Christ. Further, Incarnation always implies something about approach *by* God and *to* God, and always says something about suffering, but it does not always imply atonement, or at least not the full raft of atonement doctrines. Some of what people mean by "atonement" can be communicated by these prior categories (divinity, approach, suffering).

Belief in the Incarnation does not make inevitable the acceptance of any particular formulation of atonement. I would assert that none of the most prominent atonement teachings (those of Gregory the Great, Anselm, Luther, and Calvin) are *necessary* doctrines, but the Incarnation *is*. Without the Incarnation there is no Christianity. Atonement teachings are quite personal ideas that become attached to the central insight—the Incarnation. But why does it matter that *this* one died? Because of *who* that person was and is: the uniquely divine Son. Some concept of the Incarnation precedes all their atonement concepts, but does not supply the actual content of their atonement reasoning.

Gregory the Great says humans have sinned, so humans must offer a sacrifice, and only a human sacrifice would be sufficient.[10] Anselm has human sin putting humanity into irretrievably large debt that could only be paid by a perfectly divine human. Luther says sin caused complete alienation from God, that every individual deserves to be damned, even though he cannot *help* sinning, but that God decided to provide the means by which *some* might be saved. None of these ideas is derived from the Incarnation, though each one communicates each author's ideas about the Incarnation. None is essential to recognizing that God shares the suffering of humanity; that God, in Christ, drew very near to humanity; or that Christ endured the last full measure of painful human existence. These incarnational ideas do not require any notion of Christ as a ritual sacrificial victim, as making a payment to God, or as taking on humanity's death sentence. These notions may be common, but they turn out not to be essential to Christianity, and every theologian discards one or another of them.

---

[10] From Gregory's *Moral Teachings from Job* 17.46; cited in F. Homes Dudden, *Gregory the Great: His Place in History and Thought, vol. II* (New York: Longmans, Green, 1905) 341.

Nevertheless, the popular atonement ideas do have biblical roots, not only the individual images, but the blended ones, so it is necessary to examine the biblical roots of Christian atonement theologies.

Ritual Atonement Metaphors

Throughout the ANE, the notion of impurity (caused by both ritual and moral infractions) dominated public religious rituals. The impurity that corrupted the temples had to be cleansed, or the god would depart from the temple. In this regard, Israel's temple religion does not differ from that of Assyria, Babylon, or Canaan. This impurity was cleansed through the sacrificial cult[11] and through expulsion rituals like the scapegoat rite (see below).

English *atonement* suggests reconciliation and making up for a misdeed, not necessarily implying cult, but we should not forget that biblical atonement terms originated within a cultic arena. The verbs that most commonly underlie "atone" in English Bibles are the Hebrew *kipper*[12] and the Greek *hilaskomai* or *exilaskomai*,[13] each of which has three main usages, to signify: (1) appeasement; soothing someone's anger; (2) expiation, that is sacrificial cleansing; or (3) making amends.

The first and most important biblical source for Christian atonement doctrines is the letters of Paul the Apostle. Paul's reasoning is by no means clear to modern interpreters. Even with good background work, we find Paul difficult because he blends metaphors from the cultic, economic, and political realms, so we need to examine the logic of each metaphor separately and then see how he blends them.

Paul uses cultic and purchase metaphors to picture how the death of Jesus accomplishes salvation, and *social* metaphors to describe the saving *effects*. Paul describes Christ as a purification sacrifice (*peri hamartias*,[14] Rom 8:3); as the Paschal Lamb (1 Cor 5:7); as a new covenant

---

[11] Jacob Milgrom, *Studies in Cultic Theology and Terminology* (SJLA 36; Leiden: Brill, 1983) 69.

[12] Jacob Milgrom, *Leviticus*, Vol. 1. AB 3 (Garden City: Doubleday, 1991) 1079–83; John E. Hartley, *Leviticus*. WBC 4 (Dallas: Word Books, 1992) 64–5; Leon Morris, *The Apostolic Preaching of the Cross*. 3rd ed. (Grand Rapids, Mich.: Eerdmans, 1965) 168.

[13] Stanislas Lyonnet, "The Terminology of Redemption," in *Sin, Redemption and Sacrifice: A Biblical and Patristic Study*. Analecta Biblica 48 (Rome: Biblical Institute, 1970) 130–7; C. H. Dodd, *The Bible and the Greeks* (London: Hodder and Stoughton, 1935) 84–9; Morris, *Apostolic Preaching*, 125–6, 148, 157, 173.

[14] This is the technical term for the purification offering or sin offering (N. T. Wright, *The Climax of the Covenant: Christ and the Law in Pauline Theology* [Edinburgh: T & T Clark,

sacrifice (1 Cor 11:25); and as the *place* where sacrificial purification takes place (the *hilastērion* or mercy seat: the lid of the ark of the covenant where the sacrificial blood is sprinkled on Yom Kippur; Romans 3:25[15]).

By Paul's time, the understanding and interpretation of cult was being spiritualized—removed from the arena of bloody cult practice and reinterpreted in moral or metaphorical ways—but the atonement concept still had this cultic basis, and this is quite evident in Paul's usage.

He combines the ritual images with redemption, which is an economic notion; the Greek terms (*apolytrōsis, agorazō, exagorazō*) indicate a ransom payment for the release of captives, the purchase of slaves, or a slave's own purchase (manumission) of his freedom. Words related to *apolytrōsis* are also used to speak of the biblical Exodus. In Romans 3:24, Paul speaks of "redemption" in Christ and in the next verse of Christ as the *place* of atonement.

Paul also applies to Christ the image of a scapegoat, a more primitive practice (an "expulsion ritual") in which an animal literally bears away sin. This seems to be indicated in Paul's image of "Christ. . . becoming a curse for us" (Gal 3:13), of his being "made to be sin" (2 Cor 5:21). This is a *reversal* ritual;[16] there is an exchange of status: the pure goat (here, Christ) takes on sin, and the impure community takes on the purity of the goat, which must then be driven out of the community. I often call this type of ritual a curse transmission ritual, especially when talking about Paul, since, in five of his metaphors, he focuses on the *transfer* of sin or curse more than on the expulsion. The usual term for this kind of ritual, however, is expulsion ritual, and the scapegoat is but one example of this very widespread and ancient rite.

Expulsion ritual (very common in Greek societies) is fundamentally different from sacrifice. I will use Israel's main expulsion ritual, the scapegoat, as an example. The sacrificial animal is pure; the scapegoat starts out as pure but impurity or "transgressions" are poured upon it. The scapegoat is not an offering at all but a sin-carrier, and once the

---

1991] 222), but many English translations handle it word-for-word, yielding "regarding sin," or "to deal with sin."

[15] Peter Stuhlmacher, *Reconciliation, Law and Righteousness: Essays in Biblical Theology* (Philadelphia: Fortress, 1986) 60–2. I will give a more detailed treatment in the next chapter.

[16] Cf. Walter Burkert, *Structure and History in Greek Mythology and Ritual* (Berkeley: University of California Press, 1979) 62; Bradley Hudson McLean, *The Cursed Christ: Mediterranean Expulsion Rituals and Pauline Soteriology*. JSNT Sup 126 (Sheffield: Sheffield Academic, 1996) 74.

sins or curse are transferred to it, it must be quickly driven out of the community. I list five fundamental contrasts:

A sacrifice is pure,
—is offered up
—to Yahweh
—in a careful and controlled manner
—at the community's central sanctuary.

The scapegoat is impure,
—is not an offering or a gift,
—is not given to Yahweh,
—is ritually abused and mistreated,[17]
—and is then driven out of the sacred precincts, out of the city, into the realm of Azazel (probably a wilderness demon).

Expulsion is the opposite of sacrifice in many ways; a curse-bearer is the opposite of a precious gift. Sacrifice is more *theological*, focused on a relationship to a deity, communicated through obeisance and repentance, while the scapegoat is more *magical*, retaining primitive ideas about the literal manipulation of metaphysical reality. Most of these distinctions also hold for expulsion rituals in other cultures, but a deity is invoked in some Hittite rituals.[18] The deity has little or nothing to do with the ritual in Israel, Greece, or Mesopotamia.

The logic of scapegoat is profoundly different than the logic of sacrifice, yet the two can be conflated by a spinner of metaphors such as Paul—and this may be happening in the mixed metaphor in Romans 8:3b: "sending his own Son in the likeness of sinful flesh, and as a purification offering, he condemned sin in the flesh."[19] The condemned flesh summons up the image of the scapegoat, yet a specifically sacrificial term occurs in the verse, while the whole setting of *condemnation* is judicial. Three images are being conflated (sacrifice, scapegoat, law court). Such conflation was considered rhetorically effective and clever in the ancient world.

After the saving death of Christ come the beneficial aftereffects for believers, and Paul prefers to use *social* metaphors to describe these

---

[17] Mishnaic and early Christian sources mention the mistreatment of the scapegoat (e.g., *Yoma* 6:4; *Barnabas* 7:7-9); see the next chapter.

[18] David P. Wright, *The Disposal of Impurity: Elimination Rites in the Bible and in Hittite and Mesopotamian Literature*. SBLDS 101 (Atlanta: Scholars Press, 1987) 49.

[19] I alter the NRSV wording to bring out the sacrificial connection of *peri hamartias*.

effects: justification (acquittal), reconciliation, and adoption. "Reconciliation" uses a term *(katallagey)* that, in the Greek texts, usually refers to restoration of good relations between estranged spouses or diplomatic settlement between states.[20] "Justification" uses *dikaiosis* and related words that signify "making just," which can mean either a judicial just-making, that is, acquittal, or a moral just-making that actually transforms a person. Paul also speaks of believers being "adopted" as sons or heirs of Christ, using the legal term *(huiothesia)* for formal adoption, which really means designating a nonrelative to be an heir (Rom 8:15, 23).

The situation is further complicated by the possibility that Paul's emphasis may be heroic rather than ritual, with Christ dying a "noble death" for his friends, a major theme in Hellenic, Hellenistic, and finally Jewish (Maccabean) literature.[21] His many statements that Christ died "for us" or "for me" could be interpreted as sacrificial, as heroic, or both, since previous authors had already used cultic imagery to picture the effect of martyrs' deaths. Often one metaphor will interpret another, as we will see in the chapter on Paul.

The Logic(s) of Atonement

What does Paul's cultic and redemptive imagery mean? Does it mean Jesus' blood has purifying power, as did sacrificial blood in the Levitical cult? Does it mean the death was a kind of payment to God, as sacrifices were often understood to be? Or does it mean that he died as a substitute victim, a stand-in for guilty humans? Was sacrifice a purification, a payment, a penal substitute, or did it symbolize inward moral change? The latter seems unlikely, since that is never once mentioned in Leviticus or Numbers. Is scapegoat the fundamental image, the notion of the physical deportation of sin, or perhaps scapegoat as blended with some metaphor that adds moral meaning to it?

How did Paul really think of the death having a saving effect? Was it a ritual event, an effective martyrdom, or a trial with a last-minute substitution? If one says "it was all of these," then one leaves the logic of the transaction unexplained, for these operate by different sets of logic. Christian doctrines of atonement have in fact created a new

---

[20] H. Merkel, Καταλλάσω, κτλ in *Exegetical Dictionary of the New Testament*, vol. 2, ed. Horst Balz and Gerhard Schneider (Grand Rapids: Eerdmans, 1991) 261.

[21] Sam K. Williams, *Jesus' Death as Saving Event: The Background and Origin of a Concept*. HDR 2 (Missoula, Mont.: Scholars Press, 1975) 57–8, and throughout.

logic, combining elements from each of these underlying metaphors. The understanding of individual Christians derives from the logical assumptions underlying one or another of these metaphors. The judicial one might be the most frequent (humankind condemned, but Jesus taking on the death sentence), but it rarely functions alone; usually it is linked with one or another of the other metaphors: the sacrificial one (he was *offered* in our place), the monetary one (he *paid* the price, or penalty), or the martyrdom (he *gave himself up* in our place). It would be helpful to spell out the different assumptions upon which Christians base their diverse atonement ideas.

Paul did not initiate the sacrificial interpretation of the death of Christ,[22] but he did formulate the version that has prevailed in Christian interpretation. In so doing, he took up and transmitted a primitive current in religious thinking, but spiritualized it with an emphasis on the heroic martyrdom of Jesus and the generosity of God. Paul emphasizes the outgoing love of God, but uses metaphors that imply that the death was a payment or offering to God.

Paul's chosen emphasis on God's generosity stands in tension with what the metaphors imply. Paul argues that God is both just and merciful, but the metaphors imply a division in God's nature between justice and mercy, a need to avert wrath, a need for salvation to be "bought with a price" (1 Cor 7:23). Thus, despite his extended arguments, Paul's metaphors suggest that God is somehow manipulated, bought-off, appeased. Paul is a pragmatic preacher, and will use whatever metaphor conveys the image of Christ's self-surrender, resulting in a certain kind of transaction. The stress is on Christ's (and God's) generosity, but the metaphors hint at a payment-demanding or sacrifice-demanding God. Both ideas are often conveyed in the same passage. Through most of 2 Corinthians 5, the generosity of God is emphasized: in 5:19, "God was reconciling the world to himself" (decidedly not *being* reconciled or persuaded); yet salvation still required a ritual substitution, when God "made him to be sin who knew no sin" (v. 21). God extends forgiveness *by* and *through* this action of unloading sin onto Christ. Christ is the sacrificial gateway through which one must go in order to pass from alienation to reconciliation.

The cultic metaphors convey the idea that God chooses to *recognize* the crucifixion as an effective ritual and to respond to it. The crucifixion

---

[22] On supposed "formulas" used by Paul, see John Reumann, "The Gospel of the Righteousness of God: Pauline Interpretation in Romans 3:21-31," in *Interpretation* 20 (1966) 434–9, 450–1.

functions as the ritual act, the resurrection corresponds to God's positive response, and reconciliation and justification correspond to the transformed or cleansed status that ritual participants receive. Whether in ritual or in ritual metaphor, what is *done* evokes a desired response from God.

Some of the implications of the NT metaphors are unacceptable to many Christians and have been either criticized or (more often) spiritualized—redefined in moral and philosophic categories—from the second century to the present day. For a hundred generations, Christians have criticized, rationalized, and spiritualized the previous generations' formulations of atonement doctrine, and this process has never been more pronounced than it is today where thinkers like Weaver, Winter, and Gunton try to offer a corrected understanding of atonement but find it necessary to criticize prior formulations.

In any case, we need now to examine, at least briefly, the biblical basis of sacrifice, scapegoat, and redemption before proceeding to look at Paul in more detail, at Paul's successors, at some recent reshapings of atonement, at basic soteriology (teachings on salvation), and then at the central notion of the Incarnation. Only by learning as much as we can about the background of Paul's atonement metaphors and about the ways that his successors have adapted and added to his ideas is the scholar or believer equipped to approach this explosive subject with sufficient knowledge and, possibly, with wisdom. It is certain that "without knowledge there is no wisdom" (Sir 3:25; v. 24 in NAB). Let us "gain in learning" (Prov 9:9).

1

Sacrifice and Scapegoat

We cannot really appreciate Paul's sacrificial metaphors unless we look at Hebrew sacrifice and even at Gentile sacrifice, since Paul's successes were mainly with Gentiles, and he was very much aware of the religious ideas they held. The important idea of ritual cleansing and repair will be examined. We also will look at the critiques, rationalizations, and spiritualizing reinterpretations of sacrifice expressed by prophets and thinkers, Jewish and Gentile.

Paul uses sacrifice as one of his key metaphors for the efficacy and significance of the death of the Messiah. Nor was Paul the only person using sacrifice metaphorically. This raises the subjects of spiritualization and typology: ways in which Jews and Christians altered and reinterpreted sacrificial ritual (sections 1.2 and 1.3).

After that, expulsion rituals in Gentile and Jewish society will be examined. That enables us to make a clear distinction between the scapegoat ritual and sacrifice, noticing the very different theological assumptions that underlie the two rites. Finally we will notice how Christian scholarship and belief often blend sacrifice and scapegoat.

We are looking at the *facts* of ritual practice in Paul's world and at the wide range of differing *interpretations* of these practices so as to better approach the question of atonement in Paul as communicated by his use of ritual metaphors (examined in detail in chapter 2).

1.1 Hebrew Sacrifice

1.1.1 As a Gift

For many centuries, sacrificial practice and interpretation in Israel resembled that of Israel's neighbors: Canaanites, Moabites, Babylonians, and others. At its crudest level, the sacrificial meat is "the food of the deity."[1] The Lord calls it "My offering, the food for my offerings by fire, my pleasing odor" (Num 28:2). The priests call it "a food offering by fire to the Lord" (Lev 3:11). The "pleasing odor" *(reyach nichoach)* occurs forty-two times in the Hebrew Bible; figuratively it means a sacrifice that God accepts, but its literal and older meaning is smoke that is tasty to God. The verbal root *nuah* means rest, so it is a restful or "tranquilizing" aroma, pacifying God's anger, as shown in Genesis 8:21, where "Noah's sacrifices assuaged God's wrath."[2]

This is what the term "propitiation" means: appeasing and making peace with someone who is angry. Sacrificial ritual preserves this idea of the offering being *persuasive*[3] or even coercive, but other ideas are added to the understanding of sacrifice. The food-offering gets described with the more dignified label of *gift*,[4] thus emphasizing respect and obeisance rather than manipulation. However, we must notice that the gift still consists of the culture's best available food items, just what an anthropomorphic god (and one capable of being persuaded) would want.

1.1.2 For Purification

One of the authors (really a number of priestly authors and editors) of the Pentateuch (the first five books of the Bible) is labeled P by scholars. P is uneasy with the notion of God smelling the sacrifice,[5] "receiving pleasure from the sweet aroma."[6] P brings in a different concept: sacrifice as a kind of technology for spiritual cleansing, not for persuading God. Impurity is taken quite literally, as a stain on the sacred installations and altars of the Temple needing to be removed. God will abandon the Temple if impurity is allowed to persist.[7] Impurity stands for dis-

---

[1] Gary Anderson, "Sacrifice and Sacrificial Offerings (OT)," in *ABD* V:878. On the outgrowing of this notion, see Royden Keith Yerkes, *Sacrifice in Greek and Roman Religions and Early Judaism* (London: Adam and Charles Black, 1953) 157–8.

[2] Douglas McC. L. Judisch, "Propitiation in the Language and Typology of the OT," *CTQ* 48 (1984) 225.

[3] Morris, *Apostolic Preaching*, 167–9.

[4] Milgrom, *Leviticus*, 441.

[5] Gary Anderson, "The Interpretation of the Purification Offering חטאת *[ḥaṭṭa't]* in the *Temple Scroll* (11QTemple) and Rabbinic Literature," *JBL* 111 (1992) 27 n. 18.

[6] Israel Knohl, "The Sin Offering Law in the 'Holiness School,'" in *Priesthood and Cult in Ancient Israel*, ed. G. Anderson and S. Olyan. JSOT Sup 125 (Sheffield: Sheffield Academic, 1991) 199.

[7] Jacob Milgrom, "Kipper," in *Encyclopaedia Judaica*, vol. 10 (New York: Macmillan, 1971) 1040.

order, a kind of spiritual chaos; ritual restores purity, that is, order.[8] Sacrificial ritual, then, is seen as protective, rather than propitiatory.

Another Pentateuchal author, H (standing for the Holiness Code), repersonalizes the cultic transaction, deliberately reintroducing anthropomorphism.[9] It is the attitude of the personal God that matters most for H. The role of blood is retained but demoted in importance. The centrality of the pleasing aroma returns,[10] but to it is added the notion that the blood has a *ransoming* effect.[11] So we have three distinct concepts: sacrifice as a food-bribe (indicated by the "sweet aroma" in J); sacrificial blood as a spiritual detergent (P's purification idea); sacrifice as a ritual payment (H). Blood has literal, payment value in J and H. It has supernatural power in P and H.

H, thus, combines the viewpoints of his predecessors, and this is seen in the centrally important verse, Leviticus 17:11: "For the life of the flesh is in the blood; and I have given it to you for making atonement for your lives on the altar; for, as life, it is the blood that makes atonement."

The metaphysical logic of making atonement *because life is in the blood* is not obvious to us, though it presumably was to the original readers. Leviticus 17:14 states this slightly differently when it says, "the life of every creature is its blood," while verse 11 had said that life is a force *within* the blood. The logic that is assumed may be this: the life-force can undo, or cleanse, the death-force that is impurity. Expressed as an analogy of electricity, we can say that blood carries a life-charge that neutralizes the negative charge of the pollution.

The complicated theology of impurity and its accompanying technology of cleansing is a move away from anthropomorphism, but not an abandonment of fear and manipulation. However, now *substances* are manipulated rather than the Deity. The ritual participants still dread the possibility of the Holy One's departure from the Temple, and also worry about the danger of improprieties, large or small, in ritual procedure.

---

[8] Purity rules articulate social, and even intellectual, distinctions (Frank H. Gorman Jr., *The Ideology of Ritual: Space, Time and Status in the Priestly Theology*. JSOT Sup 91 [Sheffield: Sheffield Academic, 1990] 51). Sacrifice has to do, in part, with "correct definition, discrimination and order" (Mary Douglas, *Purity and Danger: An Analysis of Concepts of Pollution and Taboo* [New York: Frederick A. Praeger, 1966] 53).

[9] For the opinion that H is more recent than P, see Knohl, "The Sin Offering," 200, and Milgrom, *Leviticus*, 2440, 2444.

[10] Knohl, "The Sin Offering," 203.

[11] Baruch J. Schwartz, "The Prohibitions Concerning the 'Eating' of Blood in Leviticus 17," in *Priesthood and Cult in Ancient Israel*, 55, 59.

Let us define holiness. Holiness fundamentally involves the idea of *separateness*, and the separate God is dangerous and awe-some. As a sort of spiritual defense, then, ritual needed to pay special attention to boundary maintenance, expressed in terms of purity, cleansing, and separation. The priestly technology of cleansing and separation was a defense against intended or unintended provocation of the deity's wrath. It is significant that as soon as King Uzziah "became angry with the priests a leprous disease broke out on his forehead" (2 Chr 26:19). It is made clear that "the Lord had struck him" and that "he was excluded from the house of the Lord" (vv. 20-21). But the wrath of God could lash out even at people with the best of intentions, as at Uzzah, who reached out to steady the ark of the covenant when the oxen jostled it, and was then smitten dead by God (2 Sam 6:6-7). Whether one is a deliberately intrusive Uzziah or an innocent Uzzah trying to protect the ark, there is only one penalty for intrusion on divine space. If an "outsider," a non-Aaronid, approaches the incense altar, he may "become like Korah" (Num 16:40)—burnt to a cinder: "fire came out from the Lord and consumed the two hundred fifty men offering the incense" (Num 16:35). There is a narrative of divine violence upholding the mythology of holiness.

The Lord is also seen to express approval of correct sacrifice and of favored persons, answering David's sacrifice "with fire from heaven" (1 Chr 21:26), and similarly with Solomon's offering (2 Chr 7:1), but sending fire to consume Nadab and Abihu who offered up "unholy fire" (Lev 10:1), or "strange fire" (KJV), or, more accurately, "unauthorized coals."[12] Carelessness—or even ignorance—in ritual matters is fatal. It seems to be an established idea that "the glory of the Lord was like a devouring fire" (Exod 24:17).

Along with the purifying function goes forgiveness; Leviticus 4 and 5 narrate a series of sacrifices offered "on behalf" of someone, obtaining forgiveness *(salach)*,[13] which is mentioned only *after* the description of a particular act of blood-sprinkling[14] on either the altar of burnt offering, the incense altar, or the Temple curtain. The ritual was the means by which forgiveness was attained. No ritual, no forgiveness. The social

---

[12] Probably brought from a profane source, instead of from the sacrificial altar (Milgrom, *Leviticus*, 598).

[13] Judisch, "Propitiation," 226.

[14] John Dennis, "The Function of the *[ḥaṭṭaʾt]* Sacrifice in the Priestly Literature," *ETL* 78,1 (2002) 117-8; N. Kiuchi, *The Purification Offering in the Priestly Literature: Its Meaning and Function.* JSOT Sup 56 (Sheffield: Sheffield Academic, 1987) 35 n. 21.

corollary is: no professional priesthood, no forgiveness. That is why independent prophets who speak of forgiveness, like Isaiah and John the Baptist, meet strong resistance from the professional priesthood. A God who says "come, let us reason together" (Isa 1:18) can grant forgiveness without the intervention of a ritual class.

We have now mentioned the two "halves" of atonement that have been under discussion by scholars for the last two centuries, and particularly in the middle decades of the twentieth century: propitiation and expiation, which correspond to persuasion and wiping-away, and again to appeasement and cleansing. Was the sacrifice a payoff, a gift meant to soothe God's anger (propitiation), or was it a means for obtaining a sin-cleansing substance (expiation)? Most scholars would concede that both ideas are present, though they argue about which is primary and which secondary. The preponderance of opinion is that propitiation is the older idea, but that, in the P author, expiation is the primary meaning. H blends the two, stressing the life-charge that is in the blood and the restoration of relations with Yahweh.

1.1.3 Purifying the Temple

The most important sacrifices in the postexilic period are the *ḥaṭṭaʾt*, the sin-offering (Jacob Milgrom recommends "purification sacrifice" or "purification offering"), and the *ašam*, traditionally called the guilt-offering but now often designated the "reparation offering." In the Second Temple period, these sacrifices take on the cleansing or expiating function.[15] The *ḥaṭṭaʾt* is the main ritual for cleansing the Temple. It both cleanses contamination and removes blame, while the *ašam* atones for transgression on, or misuse of, Temple property.[16]

Milgrom has forced a recognition that the central cultic concern in Leviticus and Numbers is to provide ways to cleanse impurity from the Temple. Whenever sin is committed in Israel, it pollutes the Temple: "Sin is a miasma [that] is attracted to the sanctuary."[17] Deliberate sin penetrates all the way to the ark of the covenant in the Most Holy Place, and to its lid, the *kapporet*.[18] Impurity must be cleansed, principally

---

[15] A function formerly performed by the burnt-offering (Jacob Milgrom, "Further on the Expiatory Sacrifices," *JBL* 115 [1996] 513).

[16] Baruch A. Levine, *Leviticus: The Traditional Hebrew Text with the New JPS Translation* (Philadelphia: Jewish Pub. Society, 1989) 18; Milgrom, "Further," 513.

[17] Milgrom, "Kipper," 1040.

[18] Jacob Milgrom, "The Priestly Laws of Sancta Contamination," in *"Shaʿarei Talmon"*: *Studies in the Bible, Qumran, and the Ancient Near East Presented to Shemaryahu Talmon*, ed.

on Yom Kippur, the Day of Atonement, with a series of purification offerings, other sacrifices, and the scapegoat ritual. If these rituals are not
performed, God would depart from the Temple. This notion is not
unique to Israel; many ancient Near Eastern cultures had this "common obsession with temple purification."[19]

Different purifications are spelled out in the Levitical texts for handling different levels of pollution. Ḥaṭṭaʾt blood applied to the burnt offering altar purges pollution caused by the commoner's involuntary
sin; pollution caused by the high priest is cleansed by blood sprinkled
before the curtain.[20] Blood sprinkled on the *kapporet*, or mercy seat,
cleanses deliberate and wanton sin, and this can only be done once a
year, on Yom Kippur.[21] The scapegoat is said to carry away the sins and
transgressions of the people; there is no mention of impurity.[22]

Leviticus 16 describes the Yom Kippur goat purification sacrifice, the
scapegoat, the bull purification sacrifice, and two burnt offerings in suc-
cession. The two identical goats are brought forward and their eventual
fates are mentioned in verses 7-10. The bull sacrifice and the sprinkling
of its blood on the *kapporet* are described in verses 11-14, then the goat
ḥaṭṭaʾt is slaughtered and its blood sprinkled on the *kapporet* (v. 15).
Verses 16-17 narrate the reasons for the purification sacrifices—cleansing the sanctuary because of uncleanness, making atonement for the
whole assembly. Then we are told of the daubing of the bull and goat
blood on the altar of sacrifices (the "holocaust altar"). The transferring
of sins to the "live goat" (the scapegoat), and its banishment are covered in 16:20-22. After some changes of clothing and ceremonial wash-
ings, the high priest offers the burnt offerings, which have the purpose
of "making atonement for himself and for the people" (v. 24). The fat of
the (previous) purification offering is burned, the skins of the *ḥaṭṭaʾt*
animals are disposed of, the ritual ministrants undergo further wash-
ings. Verses 29-34 restate the appointed time of the holy day and some
associated rules. Atonement *(kipper)* is mentioned over a dozen times in
connection with each sacrifice, with the scapegoat, and with the whole
process, but the text focuses wholly on ritual procedure. No moral or
spiritual consequences for human beings enter the discussion in this or

---

Michael Fishbane and Emanuel Tov (Winona Lake, Ind.: Eisenbrauns, 1992) 142; Gorman,
Ideology of Ritual, 78–81.

[19] Milgrom, "Kipper," 1040.

[20] John H. Hays, "Atonement in the Book of Leviticus," *Interpretation* 52 (1998) 8.

[21] Milgrom, "Priestly Laws," 142; idem, *Studies in Cultic*, 38–41.

[22] Lev 16:21-22; Milgrom, *Leviticus*, 2445; idem, *Studies in Cultic*, 81.

the next chapter. In the next two chapters of Leviticus, leaving sacrificial ritual behind, the discussion moves on to sexual morality (ch. 18), loving one's neighbor, and showing kindness to the alien and the poor (ch. 19), and even to not harboring anger (19:17-18).

The direct concern of the priests, with ritual, was to purify the Temple and prevent the departure of Yahweh. But since it was sin that caused most of the impurity, and since the ritual is carried out "because of their transgressions, all their sins" (Lev 16:16), then we must say that the ritual also has to do with expunging sin. By cleansing the holiest symbols (the sacred installations in the Temple), the high priest is also "making atonement for himself and for the people" (Lev 16:24). Although forgiveness is not mentioned in Leviticus 16, it is probably assumed. We see seven occasions in Leviticus 4–5 where people are said to "be forgiven" (*nislach*, Lev 4:20, 26, 31, 35; 5:10, 13, 18) after cleansing rituals.

1.1.4 The Kippering of Sin

Payment is one of the base meanings of the atonement verb, *kipper*. Food has *value*. Etymologically, *kipper* "is related to *kôpher* . . . compensatory payment."[23] *Kippering* is a payoff (Num 31:50) or ransom (Exod 30:16), turning away potential retaliation (Num 8:19; 2 Sam 21:3-6).[24] Of course, in the P literature its main meaning is expiation or cleansing, both of particular Temple installations and of the individual who caused the pollution.

The *ḥaṭṭaʾt* does actually deal with sin,[25] not just with the *results* of sin, as Milgrom tries to argue when he says "the purification offering purges the sanctuary but not the wrongdoer."[26] But the sacrifice is also "for the priests and for all the people" (Lev 16:33). The key verb, *kipper*, covers more than just Temple-cleansing; the priest will "make atonement *[kipper]* . . . for all the assembly of Israel" (Lev 16:17).

The cleansing also releases the individual who caused the stain.[27] A number of scholars challenge Milgrom's tendency to minimize forgiveness.[28] When Milgrom says that one "needs forgiveness . . . because of

---

[23] Gorman, *Ideology*, 184.

[24] Milgrom, *Leviticus*, 1082–3.

[25] Dennis, "The Function," 112–7; Kiuchi, *Purification Offering*, 37, 52, 161.

[26] Milgrom, *Leviticus*, 441.

[27] Hartley, *Leviticus* 64–5; David P. Wright, "Day of Atonement," in *ABD* II (New York: Doubleday, 1992) 74; Levine, *Leviticus*, 99.

[28] Anderson, "Sacrifice (OT)," 879–80; Dennis, "The Function," 112–5, 118, 129; Kiuchi, *Purification Offering*, 62, 65, 93, 161–2; Hartley, *Leviticus*, 64.

the *consequence* of his act,"[29] he has already lost his battle to keep everything impersonal. If *forgiveness* is at issue *at all*, then more than just impersonal cleansing is going on. One can clean up a *consequence*, but only a *person* can be forgiven.

Milgrom's attempt to distance forgiveness from the ritual is motivated by his resistance to a tradition of Christianizing interpretation of the OT cult, which finds what it wants to find in the cult (transfer of sin to the animal, symbolic death of the sinner, substitutionary atonement). But Milgrom could make his valid point without creating a new one-sidedness, claiming that people are excluded from the process.

In the NT, the *hilaskomai* word-group corresponds to Hebrew *kipper*. Lyonnet defends an expiatory, that is cleansing, meaning for *hilaskomai*.[30] Dunn and Hartley make a similar observation about the Hebrew *kipper*, noting that the object of the verb is sin rather than God.[31] However, propitiation (turning away God's wrath) is an implication of the *kipper* group; many of the passages involve turning away God's anger,[32] and even Hartley reluctantly admits that the sacrifices turn away "God's . . . potential wrath."[33] Despite Hartley's resistance, this must be seen as an admission that sacrifice is propitiatory, even if it is only turning away wrath that has not *yet* manifested itself.

Propitiation is certainly present in passages where *kipper* means appeasing human wrath in Genesis 32:21; Proverbs 16:14. The crudest example is where Yahweh says that Phinehas' act of violence (killing a Hebrew and his pagan woman friend) "has turned back my wrath . . . [so that] I did not consume the Israelites" (Num 25:11). Therefore God gives him "a covenant of perpetual priesthood"; his act of violence has "made atonement for the Israelites" (Num 25:13). This is just another example of "sacred violence":[34] justifying human violence through an

---

[29] Milgrom, *Studies in Cultic,* 77; Milgrom is criticized on this point by Anderson, "Sacrifice (OT)," 880.

[30] Lyonnet, "Terminology of Redemption," 130, 137.

[31] James D. G. Dunn, *The Theology of Paul the Apostle* (Grand Rapids, Mich.: Eerdmans, 1998) 214; Hartley, *Leviticus,* 64–5.

[32] E.g., Exod 32:10-14; Num 16:45-48; Morris, *Apostolic Preaching,* 157–60; Klaus Koch, "The Translation of *kapporet* in the Septuagint," in *Pomegranates and Golden Bells,* ed. David P. Wright and others (Winona Lake, Ind.: Eisenbrauns, 1995) 68–74.

[33] Hartley, *Leviticus,* 65.

[34] "True sacrificial thinking . . . always seeks to achieve some sort of unconscious identification between the violence of the group and the figure of God" (Anthony W. Bartlett, *Cross Purposes: The Violent Grammar of Christian Atonement* [Harrisburg, Penn.: Trinity, 2001] 86).

ideology of divine violence, something that is found in any number of cultures. Israel is not unique in having this ideology, but Israel is *close* to being unique in the intensity of the critique of priestly ideology by the courageous Hebrew prophets.[35]

1.1.5 The Basic Meanings of Sacrifice

Hebrew sacrificial offerings sometimes constitute a gift, sometimes a payment, and sometimes a means for rectifying one's relationship with Yahweh. Sacrifice is fundamentally pragmatic in motivation, relating to issues of survival and well-being. In any culture, sacrificial techniques are based upon ancient metaphysical beliefs; with time, the ancient metaphysics are largely forgotten, but by then the ritual has attained such sanctity that it cannot be overthrown, though it can be changed. When changes are made in the ritual, they come from spiritualizing reflection, which is often abstract but not simply arbitrary. Spiritualization involves *evaluation* and can give new power to the symbols of the ritual. We saw that the metaphysics of sacrifice were deanthropomorphized by P and then repersonalized by H. No changes are made in the ritual or in its prevailing understanding without sufficient theological reflection and strongly felt conclusions. There is no mild opinion on sacrifice. Every critique or reinterpretation of sacrifice expresses a deeply held theological worldview.

Sacrifice is a practical system for improving the spiritual environment, originating in ancient assumptions about feeding and appeasing the god, persisting as an inscription of purity concepts, gaining further respect as a manifestation of venerable tradition, and then eliciting a multitude of reforms, critiques, and corrections.

Sacrifice is theologically interesting because it has to do with divine persons, not just with impersonal forces. This distinguishes sacrifice from expulsion ritual: the consciousness that it is conducted "before" and "for" personal gods. Sacrifice, despite its crude origins, its notion of feeding the gods, provides an arena for theological reflection.

Sacrificial cultures from Greece to Israel to India experience evolution of both the practice and the interpretation of sacrifice. There is an intensification of spiritual evaluation that leads to a sharpening of ethical sensibility, which makes blood-sacrifices look problematic. The Hebrew and Greek cultures gave rise to two different anti-sacrificial

---

[35] For instance, Isa 1:11-18; Hos 6:6-10; 8:1-13; Jer 7:22-23; and see my sections, "1.2 Spiritualization" and "4.2.2. Sacrifice as Sacred Violence."

discourses that reject or downplay the usefulness of outward ritual as compared to inward disposition and ethical behavior in society. As with the lively issues of any generation, the average person could participate in this debate. It may be that Jesus drew upon some popular anti-sacrificial, or at least anti-Temple feeling when he carried out his dramatic action in the Temple. It is said that the priests could not act against him at that time "because the whole crowd was spellbound by his teaching" (Mark 11:18); and if no one was allowed "to carry anything through the temple" (11:16), that would seem to require some popular support.

Even nineteen centuries after the cessation of the Temple sacrifices there are few theological subjects that can stir up scholarly passions more quickly than sacrifice, its critique, and its reinterpretation.

1.2 Spiritualization

Over time, and in all sacrificial cultures, one can observe the reinterpretation and alteration of sacrifice in a direction of increasingly abstract interpretation and internalization, with a tendency to go beyond the literal ritual.

The *term* spiritualization has been used by scholars to describe changes in ritual and in its interpretation. I find that the term has six meanings, both as the scholars have used it and as it may usefully be applied to analyze changes in sacrificial ritual. It can signify: (1) the progressive alteration of sacrifice through substitution and symbolization; (2) symbolic or moralizing interpretation of ritual; (3) the abstraction and internalizing of concepts (the "sacrifice [of] a broken spirit" [Ps 51:17], for instance); (4) the usage of ritual imagery to describe nonritual realities ("I am being poured out as a libation over the sacrifice . . . of your faith" [Phil 2:17]); (5) rejection of ritual, especially of bloody ritual; (6) the "making-spiritual" of personal character and motivation, a notion associated with philosophies of spiritual transformation.

1. *Alteration of ritual through substitution.* Of epochal significance was the replacement of human sacrifice with animal sacrifice. First Kings 16:34 tells of a man, apparently under the influence of Joshua's curse (Josh 6:26), sacrificing two of his sons. Such passages show there was an actual practice of sacrificing firstborn sons.[36] Psalm 106:37-40 frankly

---

[36] Jon D. Levenson, *The Death and Resurrection of the Beloved Son: The Transformation of Child Sacrifice in Judaism and Christianity* (New Haven: Yale University Press, 1993) 4–6, 20–3.

admits to the practice (in the past); Jeremiah inveighs against the practice in his time (7:30-32; 19:5; 32:35), repeatedly arguing that Yahweh never commanded it; Jeremiah finds it necessary to attack "the tradition that YHWH desires it."[37] The Bible argues against this tradition but also gives hints of its existence within Israel itself.

In the Pentateuch, Yahweh has a claim on the firstborn: "whatever is the first to open the womb among the Israelites, of human beings and animals, is mine" (Exod 13:2). This is a sacrificial claim, but Yahweh then orders that "every firstborn male among your children, you shall redeem" (Exod 13:13; cf. 34:20). Thus, the Torah indicates that Yahweh has sacrificial claims over firstborn sons and animals but orders a monetary or sacrificial substitute for the son. Levenson is not the only scholar who thinks this encodes the fact that some firstborn sons really were sacrificed, but that substitution of an animal became the norm. More shocking than Exodus 13:12-13 is Exodus 22:29 where "the firstborn of your sons you shall give to me" is *not* followed by a command to redeem the son, but by a statement equating this with the dedication of firstborn animals: "You shall do the same with your oxen and with your sheep: seven days it shall remain with its mother; on the eighth day you shall give it to me" (22:30), clearly a sacrificial instruction.[38]

The Aqedah, the story of the near-sacrifice of Isaac and its redirection at the last moment by the substitution of a ram, tells us something about the Hebrew rejection of human sacrifice but also strongly suggests an actual practice of human sacrifice. It is impossible to know how widespread child sacrifice was, but it looms in so many biblical passages that it is hard to deny its existence. The evidence (from Carthage and other societies that practiced human sacrifice) suggests that a process of animal substitution went on alongside human sacrifice.[39] Even in the Passover story there is an implied substitution: the lamb's blood allows the firstborn of Israel to be spared death (Exod 12:23-29).

Sacrificial substitutions are frequent in Greek mythology, such as a goat substituted for a boy,[40] a ram offered in place of a child, a hind substituted for Agamemnon's daughter;[41] while Hindu ritual is a vast system

---

[37] Levenson, *Death and Resurrection*, 5.

[38] Passages like this may be what Ezek 20:25 has in mind when referring to "statutes that were not good" (Levenson, *Death and Resurrection*, 4–5).

[39] Levenson, *Death and Resurrection*, 21.

[40] Pausanias 9.8.2; Dennis D. Hughes, *Human Sacrifice in Ancient Greece* (London: Routledge, 1991) 82.

[41] Hughes, *Human Sacrifice*, 83.

of substitutions for sacrifice accompanied by philosophic rationalization of substitution, eventually reaching the point that *reading* the Vedic sacrificial texts substitutes for actually carrying out a Vedic sacrifice.[42]

2. *Moralizing interpretations that insert new meanings into ritual.* This method reinterprets cult practice by attributing new and more abstract moral or universal meanings to it. Philo of Alexandria is both moralizing and universalizing when he says the priestly garments are "an 'icon' of the All," so that "the whole cosmos may perform the liturgy with" him.[43] The twelve loaves placed out during a holy day indicate "self-control, the most advantageous of the virtues."[44] The anthropologist Mary Douglas does the same thing when she says "the ritual laws . . . are grounded in justice."[45] Sometimes morality and cult are affirmed together: "Cleanse your heart from all sin. Offer a sweet-smelling sacrifice, and a memorial portion of choice flour" (Sir 38:11). Spiritualization Two is a strategy of pouring new wine into old wineskins, new values into old forms.

3. *Internalization of religion, asserting the importance of the motive, not the rite.* This kind of spiritualization "emphasiz[es] the importance of inner preparation necessary to legitimate the sacrifice."[46] "In the eyes of God it is not the number of things sacrificed that is accounted valuable, but the purity of the rational spirit of the sacrificer."[47]

The psalmist prays, "Let my prayer be counted as incense before you, and the lifting up of my hands as an evening sacrifice" (141:2). Here the right attitude *serves as*, or even replaces, the cultic action. Paul makes this point with another ritual when he speaks of "circumcision . . . of the heart—it is spiritual and not literal" (Rom 2:29, building on Deut 10:16: "Circumcise the foreskin of your heart, and do not be stubborn any longer").

There are strong moral implications to this level; Westermann says that Abraham interceding for Sodom, Moses interceding for Israel

---

[42] Brian K. Smith and Wendy Doniger, "Sacrifice and Substitution: Ritual Mystification and Mythical Demystification," *Numen* 36 (1989) 208.

[43] C.T.R. Hayward, *The Jewish Temple: A Non-biblical Sourcebook* (London: Routledge, 1996) 116 (first quoting, then paraphrasing, Philo's *Spec. Leg.* 1.96). Cf. *Mos.* II.117-18; Hayward, 113.

[44] Philo *Spec. Leg.* 1.173; translation by Hayward, *Jewish Temple*, 128.

[45] Mary Douglas, "Justice as the Cornerstone: An Interpretation of Leviticus 18–20," *Interpretation* 53 (1999) 348.

[46] Referring to Philo, is Calvin J. Roetzel, *Paul: The Man and the Myth* (Edinburgh: T & T Clark, 1999) 28.

[47] Philo, *Spec. Leg.* 1.277.

after the making of the golden calf, and Samuel interceding for Israel, all involve "a radical desacralization of sacrifice."[48] Internalizing of religious motives exalts a certain *concept* of sacrifice but reduces the importance of *literal* sacrifice. The long-term effect may be to make the literal cult irrelevant. The metaphorical value of sacrifice can be had without the literal ritual. If we are to "let thanksgiving be your sacrifice to God" (Ps 50:14 NJB), then what need is there for literal sacrifice? If the result can be obtained without the cultic act (or without the *same* cultic act), then the old cult dwindles in importance, eventually fading out of usage. This can be seen in Christianity's distance from the Temple ritual, and in Hinduism's rejection of Vedic sacrifice.

4. *Metaphorical usage of cultic terms.* This is when a cultic term is used to describe various experiences that are not within the cultic arena. Paul is the master of this kind of spiritualization, calling the body the "temple of the Holy Spirit" (1 Cor 6:19). The true circumcision are those who worship in the Spirit (Phil 3:3). Something nonarchitectural can be a temple (2 Cor 6:16). Something nonphysical can be called circumcision. If the audience is open to metaphoric expression, they understand that something spiritual (worship in the Spirit) is doing what the ritual was thought to do (demonstrate dedication to God). Level Four spiritualization often implies or leads into the next, more radical level.

5. *Rejection of sacrifice.* Open repudiation of a ritual can emerge from interiorization or from metaphorizing, from a focus on ethics or a rejection of authority structures. Since ritual encodes social boundaries and conservatism, rejection of ritual is associated with social change and reform.[49] Rejectionism became the norm among Greek philosophers. Thinkers from Heraclitus[50] to Euripides[51] to Plutarch[52] say that the real God needs no gifts.

Plato is vehement about the stupidity and impiety of thinking to manipulate the gods "by offerings and prayers"[53] that are really "offerings

---

[48] Genesis 18; Exod 32:32; 1 Sam 7:9; 12:19-25; Claus Westermann, *Isaiah 40–66* (London: SCM, 1969) 268.

[49] "All movements of religious renewal have . . . the rejection of external forms" (Mary Douglas, *Natural Symbols: Explorations in Cosmology* [New York: Pantheon, 1982] 52).

[50] James W. Thompson, "Hebrews 9 and Hellenistic Concepts of Sacrifice," in *JBL* 98 (1979) 574.

[51] The god "needs nothing" from people: Euripides, *Heracles fur.* 1341–6; cited in Helene P. Foley, *Ritual Irony: Poetry and Sacrifice in Euripides* (Ithaca, N.Y.: Cornell University Press, 1985) 163; cf. 158.

[52] Thompson, "Hebrews 9," 575.

[53] *Laws* 10.885C.

and flatteries"[54] or frankly trying to "persuade" or "bewitch" the gods[55] (an absurd notion). All that matters is the character of the one doing the offering.[56] As the "ethicizing of religion"[57] proceeds, notions of hunger, sacrifice-demanding, temper, and rage are stripped away from God, and we see the development of reflective religious philosophy that distances itself from priestly and cultic religion. Thus, Level Five spiritualization is almost always set against Level Two reformism, which is usually articulated by priests.

The radical instinct and the conservative instinct constantly struggle against each other. Yet both involve a response to rituals that have begun to seem outdated or revolting to the interpreter's contemporaries. A combination of Spiritualization Levels One (altering the ritual), Two (reinterpreting the ritual), and Three (some internalizing) is the most common strategy for handling ancient customs, making them take on new and contemporary meaning. Thus do old practices become "civilized." Most cultures prefer gradual reform to revolution, rationalization to radical rethinking. Rejection of rites seems to imply a repudiation of tradition, and so of the society that preserved the tradition. But changing and redefining religious ritual is relatively easy to pull off, even while denying that any change is taking place. Even the rhetoric of rejectionism can be subsumed in this reinterpretive process; how many rejectionist prophets have been canonized but ignored? The instinct of culture is to domesticate and neutralize every prophet. Along with this de-radicalization, however, goes a moderate reform and a gradual stressing of the inward (Level Three) and metaphorical (Level Four) significance of sacrifice. But Levels Five and Six seem threatening and complicated, respectively, and rarely win over the masses of people.

This same conservative thinking has dominated biblical scholarship on this subject for the past seventy-five years and has led to the insupportable, but commonly stated, opinion that the Hebrew prophets never attacked the cult, but only an insincere participation in it. Of course, there *are* some passages that make this point, such as Psalm 4:5 ("Offer right sacrifices and put your trust in the Lord") and Proverbs

---

[54] *Laws* 10.948C, offerings and flatteries.

[55] *Laws* 10.909B.

[56] *Alcibiades* II 149E; Everett Ferguson, "Spiritual Sacrifice in Early Christianity and Its Environment," *ANRW* 23.2:1152.

[57] R. J. McKelvey, *The New Temple: The Church in the New Testament* (Oxford: Oxford University Press, 1969) 56.

15:8 ("The sacrifice of the wicked is an abomination to the Lord, but the prayer of the upright is his delight"). But one should notice the difference between these two passages. The first one expresses support for the cult, the second one does not: it does not say the *sacrifice* of the upright is God's delight, but *prayer*. It drops sacrifice right out of the picture. There are other such aphorisms that are noticeably silent on the question of whether the cult has any value. I call the first group (like Ps 4:5 and Mal 1:6-14) *reformist* and the second group *strictly moral*. The strictly moral sayings assert a moral value while conspicuously not granting any value to sacrifice itself.

I find two kinds of statements that are even more critical of sacrifice, which I call *critical* and *radical* sayings. *Critical* sayings clearly designate righteousness as more important than cult, as in Proverbs 21:3: "to do righteousness and justice is more acceptable to the Lord than sacrifice." Unlike the strictly moral saying, this kind of saying openly designates sacrifice as *secondary*: "to obey is better than sacrifice" (1 Sam 15:22). *Radical* sayings go the furthest, ridiculing sacrifice or attacking it:

> If I were I hungry, I would not tell you, for the world and all that is in it is mine. Do I eat the flesh of bulls, or drink the blood of goats? (Ps 50:12-13)
>
> Sacrifice and offering you do not desire. (Ps 40:6)
>
> I hate, I despise your festivals. (Amos 5:21)
>
> For I desire steadfast love and not sacrifice. (Hos 6:6)
>
> Shall I come before him with burnt offerings, with calves a year old? Will the Lord be pleased with thousands of rams, with ten thousands of rivers of oil? Shall I give my firstborn for my transgression, the fruit of my body for the sin of my soul? (Mic 6:6-7)

The last saying shows a deliberate piling up of ever greater and more absurd attempts to "please" the Lord. Passages like these undermine the notion that these prophets were on the Temple's payroll, truly an attempt to "reduce the prophets to ordinariness by making them conform to somewhat conventional ideas of piety."[58] It is not true that the prophets were never disrespectful of the established cult; some passages are like *exercises* in calculated disrespect!—

> Whoever slaughters an ox is like one who kills a human being . . . whoever presents a grain offering, like one who offers swine's blood. (Isa 66:3)

---

[58] William McKane, "Prophet and Institution," *ZAW* 94 (1982) 253.

Prestigious scholars often have an instinctive dread of such radical sayings and want to see them swept under the rug. But there really is a "polemic against sacrifice and temple worship"[59] in prophets like Jeremiah and Hosea. Their main complaint is how sacrifice is used to cover up evil behavior, but this does not mean they are perfectly happy with the ritual itself. These are the two prophets who attack the belief that God had anything to do with establishing the sacrificial regime: "Did you bring to me sacrifices and offerings the forty years in the wilderness?" (Amos 5:25); "In the day that I brought your ancestors out of the land of Egypt, I did not speak to them or command them concerning burnt offerings and sacrifices" (Jer 7:22). The whole theological claim for the cult is undercut.

God's main complaint, according to Hosea, is with the priests: they reject knowledge, and so the people are destroyed (4:6). They are doing plenty of sacrificing, but really they build "altars for sinning" (8:11)! In fact, the priests "feed on the sin of my people" (4:8) and "their heart is false" (10:2). Hosea does use a cultic term when he calls Israel polluted (*nitma*ʾ, 5:3; 6:10), but he is not talking about their cultic condition but about their habitual dishonesty and violence (4:1-2) that have actually made it impossible for them to return to God (5:4).

Jeremiah makes the same point. People appeal to "the temple of the Lord . . . the temple of the Lord" (Jer 7:4), but then they "steal, murder, commit adultery" and turn the Temple into "a den of robbers" (7:9, 11). Hosea and Jeremiah use cultic terms to shock their listeners and to detach them from their false security. It is not a lack of ritual that is causing problems, but "lack of knowledge . . . hav[ing] forgotten the law of your God" (Hos 4:6). They would prefer sacrifices and eating to the actual written instructions of God (Hos 8:12-13).

Jesus shares the prophetic radical attitude,[60] quoting Hosea's and Micah's most radical statements (Matt 9:13; 12:7; 23:23) and one of Jeremiah's anti-Temple remarks (Matt 21:13). Elsewhere in the Gospels, however, Jesus seems to fit into the "strictly moral" category, making his views clear but not picking a fight with the cult as he seems to do in the Gospel of Matthew. In all the Gospels, however, Jesus emphasizes

---

[59] McKane, "Prophet and Institution," 259.

[60] Frances M. Young, "Temple Cult and Law in Early Christianity: A Study in the Relationship between Jews and Christians in the Early Centuries," *NTS* 19 (1972–3) 336; J. McGuckin, "Sacrifice and Atonement: An Investigation into the Attitude of Jesus of Nazareth towards Cultic Sacrifice," in *Remembering for the Future*, ed. Yehuda Bauer and others (Oxford: Pergamon, 1989) 1:649.

the inner attitude and has no patience with outward posturing, and that is thoroughly in the spirit of Hosea and Micah.

Of course, some biblical passages show signs of fitting into more than one of my categories. Isaiah 1 makes a reformist statement ("I cannot endure solemn assemblies with iniquity," 1:13b), but also numerous radical ones ("I have had enough of burnt offerings of rams and the fat of fed beasts . . . . incense is an abomination to me," 1:11, 13a).

Some early Christians were very anti-cultic, in particular, the Ebionites. Although they sometimes refer to sacrifice metaphorically,[61] they strongly reject the notion of Christ as a sacrifice,[62] referring to the Pauline notion of the Eucharist as "to drink the blood of corpses."[63] The so-called *Epistle of Barnabas* is another document that takes a fundamentally negative attitude toward Jewish rituals[64] yet engages in some metaphorical uses of certain rites, understanding the scapegoat to be a prefiguration of the death of Christ.[65] Therefore, it is not very helpful to say that "spiritualization of the cult recognizes the axiomatic nature of the sacrificial cult"[66] unless one means recognizing the *rhetorical*, and not necessarily any literal, usefulness of the cult. "Feeding on sin" and "altars for sinning" (Hos 4:8; 8:11) concede only rhetorical, not actual, value to the cult.

6. *Spiritualization as transformation.* Here, "spiritualization" means "to make spiritual," joining the ethical and philosophic insights of Levels Three and Four, and usually adding the rejectionism of Level Five, issuing in a philosophy of spiritual progress. Middle Platonic and Stoic philosophies generally reflect this kind of religious thought, though Stoicism lacks a very useful theological vocabulary. Somewhat more developed theologically was Hermeticism, a Gnostic philosophy that articulated internalization, metaphor, and spiritual transformation. The Hermetic philosophy rejected literal sacrifice[67] but used the concept metaphorically. A key Hermetic phrase was "rational sacrifice," meaning prayer.[68] Paul echoes Hermetic terminology when he exhorts

---

[61] In a work that has not, to my knowledge, been fully translated into English, Jesus says "I will become an altar for them" (*Testament of our Lord Jesus in Galilee* 7; in John J. Gunther, *St. Paul's Opponents and Their Background: A Study of Apocalyptic and Jewish Sectarian Teachings.* NovTSup 35 [Leiden: Brill, 1973] 151).

[62] Hans-Joachim Schoeps, "Ebionite Christianity," *JTS* n.s. 4 (1953) 221–2.

[63] *Testament of our Lord* 7; Gunther, 151.

[64] It equates Jewish observances with idolatry: *Barn.* 4:7; 9:4-6; 16:1-5.

[65] "The other goat . . . Jesus is prefigured by it!" (*Barn.* 7:7).

[66] Roetzel, *Paul*, 192 n. 93.

[67] Young, "Temple Cult and Law," 328, referring to *Corpus Hermeticum* 1.31; 12.23; 13.21.

[68] Ferguson, "Spiritual Sacrifice," 1154; see *CH* 13.18-19.

the Romans to "present your bodies as a living sacrifice, holy and acceptable to God, which is your spiritual worship" (Rom 12:1). Similar views had been expressed in the Hellenistic Jewish work *Testaments of the Twelve Patriarchs*, where the angels offer "a rational and bloodless oblation" in heaven.[69] Paul can draw upon Jewish or Gentile spiritualizing traditions without having to directly quote any source, and one can discern in Paul a program for "a total spiritualization of reality."[70]

Christian philosophies that articulate Level Six Spiritualization often express it in terms of *theōsis* or divinization, sometimes building upon 2 Peter 1:4: "[we] may become participants of the divine nature," or upon Matthew 5:48: "be perfect, therefore, as your heavenly Father is perfect." The nineteenth- and twentieth-century philosopher Vladimir Soloviev is a good example of modern thinking on *theōsis*; he speaks of "a universal *restoration* of all things . . . . in which God is all in all . . . . a changing of bodily life . . . in which all creation becomes a faithful likeness of the Godhead."[71] "The soul [is] the spirit in the process of being realized."[72]

Such a notion of progressive perfection or transformation, of becoming spiritual, is the crowning phase of spiritualization. The reader by now has probably noticed that I am doing more than describing how this term has been used by scholars and theologians. I am also arguing that there is a process of evolution of spiritual philosophy that can be discerned in many cultures, culminating in a Level Six philosophy of spiritual progress, which usually involves some distance from cultic usages of the past. The slogans of this level of thought are: do the will of God, abandon superstition, participate in divinity, take on the divine nature. Here, the message of Jesus is understood to speak of the transformation of human character into the likeness of God's character, and this becomes the goal of religious living.

In summary, spiritualization describes the transformation and eventual abandonment of sacrifice, through substitution, moralizing, interiorization, metaphor, rejectionism, and philosophic reflection that shifts

---

[69] *T. Levi* 3:6; *The Old Testament Pseudepigrapha*, ed. James H. Charlesworth (New York: Doubleday, 1983) 789; cf. McKelvey, *New Temple*, 31–2.

[70] Paul Ciholas, "Knowledge and Faith: Pauline Platonisms and the Spiritualization of Reality," *PRSt* 3 (1976) 199.

[71] Vladimir Soloviev (here spelled Solovyev), *God, Man and the Church: The Spiritual Foundations of Life*, trans. Donald Attwater (London: James Clarke, 1938) 134, 168.

[72] Vladimir Soloviev, *Lectures on Divine Humanity*, trans. Peter Zouboff, revised by Boris Jakim (Hudson, N.Y.: Lindisfarne, 1995) 101. The lectures were delivered from 1878 to 1881.

the focus of religion toward spiritual transformation. The six levels of spiritualization record a process of transformation through symbolization, and this applies to religious ideas as well as to rituals. Spiritualization is a response to an inward (moral) and outward (developmental) pressure for change. It demonstrates a gradual ascendancy of religious values over cultic observance. I assert that the spiritualization process is a response to a genuine spiritual mandate.

Christian thought has had a complicated stance on this subject, almost always seeing OT cultic practices as prophetic of the Messiah's death, but unsure about the legitimacy of the cult itself. Christian works that directly attack the Jewish cult (*Barnabas*, Ebionite works) fail to make it into the canon. Paul teaches both supersession and fulfillment. He sees both "death" and "glory" in the Mosaic system (2 Cor 3:6-7); the "glory" of the old covenant is "now set aside" (2 Cor 3:7, 11); the "greater glory" is in the new covenant, the "permanent" covenant (3:10, 12). Reading the OT without knowing who the Messiah is, is like reading with a veil over one's head; "only in Christ is it set aside" (2 Cor 3:14).

1.3 Typological Interpretation

This puts us squarely onto the important subject of typology: reinterpreting an OT narrative so that the story is seen as a *prefiguration* or *type* (the Greek word *typos* means "stamp") of a later story or event. The type was a hint, a pattern, a promise, of some reality to come. "For whatever was written in former days was written for our instruction" (Rom 15:4). For instance, Paul sees Abraham's faith as prefiguring the faith of believers. Abraham is a *type*, a foreshadowing, of the Christian (Rom 4). Typology treats a story or an object as symbolic as well as real. Its symbolic function was to prefigure something that has come or is to come. The antitype, the fulfillment, is more real or more meaningful than is the type. This may sound like Platonic allegory but it has a fundamental difference. Allegory sees a "higher" reality imperfectly reflected or concealed in the story. This renders the original, literal story superficial. Typology does not have this distaste for the literal meaning, but it does add another meaning to the literal. Typology sees God acting again as God had acted before.

Allegory is fundamentally a Middle Platonic or Hellenistic way of thinking, seeing the material level as inferior. Allegory distinguishes *levels* (which could be called a spatial distinction), while typology makes a temporal correlation: the *earlier* prefigures the *later*. Thus, allegory involves making a *contrast*, while typology makes a *connection*. Allegory says, "this is not really this; it is something else." Typology says, "this is that[73] which was spoken of by the prophet."

Paul can serve as our example of a typological interpreter, as when he pictures Abraham as a *type* of the faithful believer. Philo of Alexandria can be our allegorical thinker. Philo says Abraham's decision to leave Ur stands for the rational mind turning away from the sensual life—"he means by Abraham's country the body, and by his kindred the outward senses."[74] The geography and persons of the original story are irrelevant; only the supposed turning away from the senses is important (this man with wives and concubines!).

Both typological and allegorical methods of interpretation look for a meaning other than the story's literal meaning, but their assumptions are profoundly different. Typology incorporates an instinct about the prophetic role of biblical texts; it turns even Genesis into a prophetic narrative. Allegory, on the other hand, turns every text into a code for a multileveled universe, with the mental or abstract level being far more meaningful than the physical or literal level. As allegory discounts the importance of the material level, so it also discounts the literal meaning; only the ignorant are attached to the literal meaning. Typology values the literal meaning of the narrative but considers its prophetic meaning to be more important.

Paul says that the story of Sarah and Hagar is an allegory, that the mountain of Sinai stands for Hagar, for ignorance, and an enslaved mind; while the mount of Jerusalem stands for Sarah, for truthful perception, and for freedom (Gal 4:24). But even this has typological implications: Sarah is a type of the Christ-believer; Hagar is a type of the unbelieving Jew.

Paul not only interprets OT types, he sometimes sees the antitype in the type. Regarding the water-bearing rock that appeared to the Israelites in the desert, Paul says "the Rock was Christ" (1 Cor 10:4). And when Moses and his followers passed through the sea, they were "baptized" in it (10:2). Thus, Christianity was already present in embryonic form in the OT.

There is a certain balance in Paul's approach that keeps it from either hostility to the old covenant or dependence upon familiar understandings of the old covenant. The same can be said of his attitude

---

[73] Borrowing from the title of a book by F. F. Bruce, *This Is That: The New Testament Development of Some Old Testament Themes* (Exeter, U.K.: Paternoster Press, 1968).

[74] *Mig.* 2.7, 10.

toward cult: he is not dependent on the old, but he does base his soteriology on a typological reinterpretation of the old cult. He thus creates a new kind of cultic ideology, spelling out how baptism is a ritual death and rebirth, while the Eucharist is taking Christ into oneself. He does not invent the Christian cult, but he gives it an interesting interpretation, one that seems to have caught on. When Paul says, "our paschal lamb, Christ, has been sacrificed" (1 Cor 5:7), he is saying the Passover lamb was a type of Christ; presumably, Christ's blood acts to avert destruction from believers.

Paul's version of the Eucharist adds prophetic words to cultic ideology; he puts Jeremiah's "new covenant" (*diathēkē kainē*, Jer 31:31 LXX) into his "new covenant in my blood" (*hē kainē diathēkē estin en tō emō haimati*, 1 Cor 11:25).[75] Thus does Paul build on tradition, encircling his message with antiquity, allowing the type to define the antitype, the cultic to express the personal. Paul does not *break* with the past but transforms it and lets it speak for the present. His metaphors are more than just vehicles for a message, they provide content to the message as well. Even if he means to say that the *whole* purpose of the sacrificial and scapegoat cults was to prefigure the death of Christ, people will then conceptualize the significance of Christ's death in terms of their concept of what these ritual events accomplished. The end result is that Christians have accepted that the death of Christ *was* a ritual event, *was* a costly payment; it was not just *like* these things.

Paul also applies typology to expulsion rituals, of which the scapegoat ritual is the main Jewish example. Since he is conscious of writing to both Jews and Gentiles, and these rites existed in both communities, he avoids all technical terms but does indicate that Jesus is the new expulsion victim. First we must examine the rituals themselves.

1.4. Expulsion Rituals

Many cultures in the ancient Near East utilized expulsion rituals. I refer to these as "curse transmission rituals" when I want to focus on the moment of the *transfer* of curse or sin onto the victim, which is what Paul seems to be focusing on in four or five soteriological passages. He also uses the scapegoat image in two passages that are not soteriological.

---

[75] I treat 1 Cor 11:23-25 as Paul's composition, although he is undoubtedly inheriting some of the wording from the Antioch Christians who trained him. Paul makes sure the wording reflects his own cultic theology, his interpretation of baptism and Eucharist as participation in the death and resurrection of the Messiah.

Bradley McLean has written a useful book that asserts that scapegoat is the *only* soteriological image used by Paul. This one-sided thesis is relatively easily to overturn, yet his work is quite useful, especially when combined with that of other scholars on expulsion ritual.

The curse transmission ritual involves the expulsion of an evil, a disease, or a curse from the community by transferring it to a victim that will act as a carrier, literally taking the evil *out* of the community. Expulsion rituals are carried out before battles (Hittites), to deport diseases (Hittites and Greeks), or to dispel sin on the highest of holy days (Israel). They seem to come from a very ancient stratum of religious thought. As we examine this ritual, we will continually observe ways in which it profoundly differs from sacrifice. Let us begin with the Gentile rites.

1.4.1 Gentile Expulsion Rites

Probably the majority of Paul's readers were Gentiles, and he was skillful at using imagery that they would recognize, although he never treated their religious traditions as normative—as genuinely God-given.

It turns out there were deep and widespread traditions of expulsion ritual in Hittite, Greek, and Mesopotamian societies. The Galatians of Paul's day were partly descended from the Hittites. Several Hittite elimination rites were designed to drive a plague out of the army using a sheep, a bull, a male prisoner, and a woman. It was assumed that the disease was caused by a god, and the persecuting god is asked to be appeased with these victims.[76] A mouse was used to carry away a disease in the Hittite Ambazzi ritual: "Let this mouse take [the evil] to the high mountains."[77] By Paul's time, Hittite society had been absorbed into several Hellenistic societies, and we no longer see most of these rites, but Galatian society in Paul's time had legal forms that incorporated expulsion and curse imagery. Curses carried both a spiritual and judicial force in Galatian society, including protective inscriptions, pillars that bore a protective curse, judicial prayers, curses as legal briefs, and confession inscriptions by those who suspected that a curse might have been filed against them.[78]

---

[76] Wright, *Disposal*, 46, 50–7. The element of "concretization" and transfer is discussed on 41–2, 48, 52.

[77] Wright, "Day of Atonement," 74.

[78] Susan Margaret Elliott, "The Rhetorical Strategy of Paul's Letter to the Galatians in Its Anatolian Cultic Context: Circumcision and the Castration of the *Galli* of the Mother of the Gods." Ph.D. dissertation, Loyola University Chicago (1997) 160–90, 639.

The ancient Greeks made frequent use of a *pharmakos*, a human scapegoat. A victim was selected, consecrated, cursed, ceremonially abused, and driven out of town.[79] At Colophon, a particularly ugly man was designated a *pharmakos*, was feasted, then ritually whipped with fig branches and driven out of town.[80] At Athens, two undesirables or prisoners were "garlanded with a string of figs, and expelled."[81] Similar rituals are attested in numerous other Greek cities. The citizens believed they were "purifying" the city of disease[82] or curse.[83] The phases of the ritual can be described as "selection . . . communication . . . separation,"[84] or as selection, consecration, investiture, transference, and expulsion.[85]

Such a human scapegoat in Greek-speaking societies could also be called a *perikatharma* or *peripsēma*,[86] both of which mean "off-scourings" or "refuse,"[87] although they can also signify a price or ransom, as in Proverbs 21:18[88] and Tobit 5:19.[89] Paul applies both these terms to himself and his fellow apostles in 1 Corinthians 4:13, who "have become like the rubbish of the world, the dregs of all things." In Corinth, his readers would likely recognize the reference to Gentile religion even though the words had evolved toward a more pedestrian meaning, as terms of polite "self-abasement."[90] It is not a coincidence that Paul chooses words that have cultic connotations. In his mind, an apostle has to suffer as a scapegoat of the world, just as Jesus did. For Paul, this is the Gospel pattern, and apostles replicate it; even ordinary believers may have to replicate it. This is also Paul's social commentary, his observation of how the ignorant world treats apostles.

---

[79] Jane Ellen Harrison, *Prolegomena to the Study of Greek Religion* (Cambridge: Cambridge University Press, 1903) 96–106; McLean, *Cursed Christ*, 73–6, 88–98.

[80] Walter Burkert, *Greek Religion: Archaic and Classical*, trans. John Raffan (Oxford: Blackwell, 1985) 82.

[81] Walter Burkert, *Structure and History in Greek Mythology and Ritual* (Berkeley: University of California Press, 1979) 65.

[82] McLean, *Cursed Christ*, 89–90, 210.

[83] Martin Hengel, *The Atonement: The Origins of the Doctrine in the New Testament* (London: SCM, 1981) 25; McLean, *Cursed Christ*, 71–2, 210.

[84] Burkert, *Structure and History*, 67.

[85] McLean, *Cursed Christ*, 73–5.

[86] Gustav Stählin, "*peripsēma*" *TDNT* 6:84, 85; Robert Parker, *Miasma: Pollution and Purification in Early Greek Religion* (Oxford: Clarendon, 1983) 24, 219, 258–9, 299; Hengel, *Atonement*, 27.

[87] *BAGD*, 647.

[88] Joseph Henry Thayer (trans. and enlarged), *A Greek-English Lexicon of the New Testament* (from Grimm) (4th ed.; Edinburgh: T & T Clark, 1901) 503.

[89] *BAGD*, 653.

[90] Stählin, *TDNT* 6:89.

1.4.2 OT Expulsion Rituals

There are OT patterns underlying some of Paul's soteriological metaphors. Particularly in 2 Corinthians 5:21 and Galatians 3:13 it seems evident that he is referring to the most important expulsion ritual in the Jewish tradition, the scapegoat ritual. Three Romans passages seem to show a scapegoat pattern as well.

Yom Kippur was Israel's most important day for riddance of sin. Of the two goats brought before the high priest Aaron, one is slain as a sin offering. It is the other one, the "live goat," that is expelled. Aaron shall press both hands on the head of the live goat and then "confess over it all the iniquities of the people of Israel, and all their transgressions, all their sins, putting them on the head of the goat, and sending it away into the wilderness" (Lev 16:21). The goat is sent to the realm of the a wilderness demon,[91] Azazel (16:26), the appropriate destination for something full of sin and death.

When the priest lays his hands on the scapegoat, "hands" is plural (Lev 16:21). In the case of a sin or purification sacrifice, it is the person who brings the animal to the priest who lays his "hand" on its head, and the noun is always singular, so we have two important differences. Laying one hand on one's own animal probably signifies only *whose* the animal is.[92] Looking at both Hittite and Hebrew rituals, David Wright says that the laying on of a single hand merely identifies from whom the offering comes.[93]

The laying on of both hands seems to signify that something is transferred, like the authority transferred by Moses to Joshua in Deuteronomy 34:9. By laying both hands on the goat and confessing sins over it, Aaron is "*putting* them on the head of the goat, and *sending* it away. . . . The goat shall *bear (naśaʾ)* on itself all their iniquities to a barren region" (Lev 16:21-22). The Hebrew verbs for literally putting (*natan*), sending (*šilaḥ*), and bearing (*naśaʾ*) are used.

Such a *literal* "putting" and "bearing" of sin is a "magical transfer,"[94] not a judicial solution. There is no court case here, there is a magical transfer and transportation. By "magic" I mean the physical manipu-

---

[91] Milgrom, *Studies in Cultic*, 81.

[92] M. C. Sansom, "Laying on of Hands in the Old Testament," in *Expository Times* 94 (1983) 325.

[93] Wright, *Disposal*, 54; idem, "The Gesture of Hand Placement in the Hebrew Bible and in Hittite Literature," *JAOS* 106 (1986) 443.

[94] Bernd Janowski, *Sühne als Heilsgeschehen: Studien zur Sühnetheologie der Priesterschrift und zur Wurzel KPR im Alten Orient und im Alten Testament* (WMANT 55; Düsseldorf: Neukirchener Verlag, 1982) 210, and again on 219.

lation of metaphysical forces or spiritual conditions. Sin here receives a naturalistic, not a moral, solution. There is only a blanket transference of sin;[95] the action does not substitute for *particular* transgressors and does not adjudicate individual sins or sinners.

The same notion of physical transfer is encountered in the ritual for cleansing a leper and the house in which a leper lives. A bird is slain and a second bird is dipped in the blood of the first and the blood is sprinkled on the leper, after which the bird is released (Lev 14:4-7). A nearly identical rite is performed with two birds and a sprinkling on the leper's house in Leviticus 14:49-53. These rituals blend sacrifice and expulsion, but the latter is dominant. The scapegoat-like idea of physical transfer is distinctly observable. The second bird, by contact with the first one's blood, presumably takes on either the leprosy or its cause and carries it away. This implies that the leprosy or its cause had already been transferred to the first bird, the sacrificial bird. The infamous contagiousness of leprosy enables *transmission* to a sacrificial victim, something otherwise only occurring with expulsion victims, not sacrificial victims; and even here, it occurs within the context of an expulsion ritual.

The scapegoat ritual is much more dramatic and public, occurring on the most holy day. It involves something that never happens with the sacrificial animal: a sort of controlled mob frenzy, with cruelty to the animal. The goat has its hair pulled by the "common people" as it is led away;[96] it is buffeted about and mistreated,[97] spat upon and stabbed,[98] and is driven out.

I disagree with those who say that the scapegoat is just another form of the sin offering,[99] or that the body of the sacrificial animal "embod[ies] the sin of the one who offered it.[100] Such assimilation of scapegoat to sacrifice imposes Christian notions of substitutionary atonement onto these rituals. It ignores the fact that the sacrificial animal did not become a sin-bearer, but was pure, and its blood was used to cleanse

---

[95] T. H. Gaster, "Sacrifices and Offerings, OT," in *The Interpreter's Dictionary of the Bible* (New York: Abingdon, 1962) 4:153.

[96] The Mishnah tractate *Yoma* 6:4; see Lester L. Grabbe, "The Scapegoat Tradition: A Study in Early Jewish Interpretation," *JSJ* 18 (1987) 158.

[97] Daniel Stökl Ben Ezra, *The Impact of Yom Kippur on Early Christianity: The Day of Atonement from Second Temple Judaism to the Fifth Century.* WUNT 163 (Tübingen: Mohr Siebeck, 2003) 31, 157–9.

[98] *Barn.* 7:8; Tertullian, *Adv. Marcion* 3.7.7 (also called *Adv. Jud.* 14.9); Grabbe, "Scapegoat," 162.

[99] Such as Dunn, "Paul's Understanding," 45, and Kiuchi, *Purification Offering*, 164.

[100] Dunn, *Theology*, 219.

the Temple. (How could sin-saturated blood cleanse a holy place?) The scapegoat comes closer to "embodying" sin, but it really is a sin-*porter*. Sacrifice and scapegoat utilize completely different kinds of metaphysical logic. There is no single category of "atoning substitution" into which these different OT rituals fit.

In fact, neither sacrifice nor scapegoat involves punishment in Leviticus. Sacrifice is fundamentally meant to purify, first the Temple and then (by implication) people. Leading scholars on the subject of expulsion ritual emphasize that the scapegoat "is in no way punished in place of the guilty. . . . Its task is confined to transport";[101] it is not a penal substitute.[102]

Yet Paul applies both rituals as metaphors for the significance of the death of Jesus. This imaginative leap may be effective in a sermon, but it does not mean that scholars no longer need to distinguish different kinds of rituals. If Paul deliberately conflates these concepts in his sermons, that can be analyzed *as a conflation*, but it does not retroactively turn the biblical scapegoat into a sacrifice.

If we are to understand Paul's mixing of metaphors, we need to understand the differences between the models that he mixed. In Romans 3:24-25 he mixes ransoming, acquittal before God, and purification at the mercy seat; this does not mean that he saw no difference between hostage-release, a law court, and temple-purification. He knows that these are different things but he mixes these metaphors and so conveys a powerful message about the death as liberating, releasing, and purifying, and as a typological fulfillment of various rituals and events in Israel's history. However, we miss the point if we think that, to start with, there is no difference between ransoming, trying in court, and purifying a temple.

Similarly, we need to distinguish expulsion rituals from sacrifice. A sacrificial animal is a gift; a curse transmission victim is a sin-carrier, not a gift (would one offer a gift to a wilderness demon?). The sacrificial animal remains pure; the scapegoat starts out pure,[103] but is made "utterly impure"[104] and does not "rate as a sacrifice."[105] The sacrifice

---

[101] Schenker, *Versöhnung und Sühne*, 115–6.

[102] Wright, "Day of Atonement," 74.

[103] Robert J. Daly, S.J., *Christian Sacrifice: The Judaeo-Christian Background Before Origen* (Washington: The Catholic University of America Press, 1978) 104.

[104] Harrison, *Prolegomena*, 101; cf. Sansom, "Laying on of Hands," 324.

[105] Milgrom, *Leviticus*, 441.

has its end in a solemn moment within the sanctuary, but the scapegoat meets its end in a frenzied mob action where it is driven out with wild abandon. Scapegoat carries out a crude enforcement of the community boundary, as though to say, "curse *out*, population *in*." It seeks spiritual rescue by material means, treating sin like a physical thing. Sacrifice shows more sensitivity to the moral dimension of sin, cleansing sin's stain from something that stands for the community (the shrine). Of course, there is also a kind of spiritual materialism in sacrifice as well, if there is a *stain* that can be literally *cleansed*. Nevertheless, sacrifice shows a higher moral consciousness in that the community needs to be made a clean place in which the Deity can dwell.

If we are to understand Jewish theology, we must distinguish sacrifice from scapegoat just as surely as we distinguish Yahweh from Azazel and differentiate the community's temple from the extracommunal wilderness. English language scholars would do well to note that most German scholars have retained a clear understanding of the difference between the metaphysics of sacrifice and those of scapegoat.[106]

1.5 Using Scapegoat to Christianize Sacrifice

Now it is possible to return to sacrifice and to Paul's metaphor in Romans 3:25 and to make some important observations. Because of how deeply ingrained is Christian substitutionary thinking, scholarship has often interpreted Hebrew sacrifice through Christian lenses. First, scapegoat themes are imported into the interpretation of sacrifice, then the burden bearing is turned into *penalty*-bearing. Heroic martyrology is added, and Christian ideas are imposed upon Hebrew sacrifice. The animal is said to become "sin-laden. . . . The animal had to be holy . . . so that . . . the death it died was *not its own*. . . . The equivalence between offerer and sacrifice lay exclusively in the *blood* of the victim."[107] The blood, then, would be polluted, but the OT says the *Temple* is polluted, and the blood cleans it up. This is not infected blood, but purifying blood; its inherent life-force cleanses the sin-pollution. Nothing bad has been transferred to the blood.

---

[106] Janowski, *Sühne*, 209–21; Gese, *Biblical Theology*, 112; Ina Willi-Plein, *Opfer und Kult im alttestamentlichen Israel: Textbefragungen und Zwischenergebnisse* (Stuttgart: Verlag Katholisches Bibelwerk, 1993) 105–6; Schenker, *Versöhnung und Sühne*, 115–9; Wolfgang Kraus, *Der Tod Jesu als Heiligtumsweihe: Eine Untersuchung zum Umfeld der Sühnevorstellung in Römer 3,25–26a* (WMANT 66; Düsseldorf: Neukirchener Verlag, 1991) 45–57, 69–70.

[107] Dunn, *Theology*, 221.

Further, the Levitical texts do not treat the slaying of the animal as the crucial moment; they focus on the careful differentiation (using six different verbs[108]) of pouring, daubing, draining, squeezing, sprinkling, or splashing the blood on the sacrificial altar, the incense altar, the Temple curtain, or the mercy seat, depending on the different kinds of sin and the different people who sinned. This has nothing to do with punishing the animal but with the purifying power that lifeblood is thought to have.

The animal is not killed in order to punish it but to get access to its blood. Milgrom's theory that the blood cleanses impurity from various Temple fixtures polluted by particular kinds of impurity makes sense of this; penal substitution does not. Standard Christian scholarship has imported more penal meaning into Paul's metaphor of Christ as the mercy seat in Romans 3:25 than is warranted. This is not to deny that Paul uses judicial and penal images, but to accurately illuminate the background of this particular Pauline passage, which is what we should do with each passage.

---

[108] Wright, *Disposal*, 147–8.

2

Paul's Use of Cultic Imagery

Paul uses multiple metaphors and models to illustrate the meaning of the death of Christ: sacrificial sprinkling, sin-bearing scapegoat, heroic martyrdom functioning as a redemption payment. Too many scholars attempt to force Paul to use only one soteriological metaphor or model: scapegoat (McLean[1]), martyrology (Sam Williams [at least, at the time he wrote his dissertation][2]), participation in Christ (Sanders[3]). Stowers allows two models: martyrology and enfranchisement in Abraham's family.[4]

But this is a rigid understanding not just of Paul but of metaphorical language. All that is needed for a metaphor to be effective is one point of contact. There is "blood" in a sacrifice and in a political murder; this enables the murder of Jesus to be compared to sacrifice, and it allows the ritual's theological implications to be imported into an interpretation of the murder. But that does not mean that other metaphors cannot be used. Paul is willing and able to use more than one metaphor—and usually in the same sentence!

2.1 The Sacrificial Metaphor in Romans 3:25

In one of his most densely packed sentences, Paul combines redemption and sacrificial metaphors for the death of Jesus, with a judicial model for its beneficial aftereffect: justification or making-right of

---

[1] McLean, *Cursed Christ*, 48.

[2] Sam K. Williams, *Jesus' Death as Saving Event: The Background and Origin of a Concept.* HDR 2 (Missoula, Mont.: Scholars, 1975) 40–1, 56–9, 233, 252.

[3] E. P. Sanders allows but minimizes sacrificial imagery, while exalting the participationist image (*Paul and Palestinian Judaism* [Philadelphia: Fortress, 1977] 463–9, 506–7, 511).

[4] Stanley K. Stowers, *A Rereading of Romans: Justice, Jews, and Gentiles* (New Haven, Conn.: Yale University Press, 1994) 227–30. On 206–13 he denies that Paul uses a sacrificial metaphor (though on 211 he allows it), and denies that sacrifice entails atonement (yet allows the possibility on 213).

believers. Unfortunately, the best scholarship on *hilastērion* is very recent and no published translation incorporates it, but NAB does a fairly decent job with the passage:

> They are justified freely by his grace
>   through the redemption (*apolytrōsis*) in Christ Jesus,
>   whom God set forth as an expiation (*hilastērion*), through faith,
>   by his blood, to prove his righteousness because of
>   the forgiveness of sins previously committed. (Rom 3:24–25 NAB)

Apolytrōsis refers to the ransoming of captives,[5] the purchasing of slaves, and the manumitting of slaves (buying their freedom).[6] In the LXX, some words related to this word are used to stress the *fact* of deliverance rather than the economic *means* of delivery.[7] Nevertheless, the secular Greek meaning of *apolytrōsis* (payment) "should be retained."[8]

Paul links his economic metaphor with a sacrificial one. The Hebrew *kapporet*, Greek *hilastērion,* sometimes called the "mercy seat" in English, is the top-piece of the ark of the covenant[9] located in the Holy of Holies (the innermost chamber in Moses' tabernacle and in the Jerusalem temples). No one could enter this chamber but the high priest, and only on Yom Kippur. The *hilastērion* was made of gold, its upper part carved into the form of a pair of cherubim with wings stretching over the ark of the covenant (Exod 25:17-22; 1 Chr 28:18).

The *hilastērion* is the place where the impurity resulting from the sins of Israel is ritually cleansed once a year, on Yom Kippur, the Day of Atonement. Blood is sprinkled on the mercy seat on this most important of holy days. So what Paul is saying is that God has put forward Christ as "mercy seat of faith" *(hilastērion dia tēs pisteōs)*, not "an expiation" (NAB). Nor does he say "sacrifice of atonement" (NRSV, NIV), or equate Jesus with the sacrificial victim (in *this* passage). A sacrificial animal may be called a *hilasmos*, as in 1 John 2:2, but it is never, in all of Greek and Jewish-Greek literature, called a *hilastērion*; rather,

---

[5] James D. G. Dunn, *Romans 1–8.* WBC 38A (Dallas: Word, 1988) 169; idem, *Theology,* 227.

[6] David Hill, *Greek Words and Hebrew Meanings: Studies in the Semantics of Soteriological Terms* (Cambridge: Cambridge University Press, 1967) 76; Morna D. Hooker, *Not Ashamed of the Gospel: New Testament Interpretations of the Death of Christ* (Grand Rapids, Mich.: Eerdmans, 1994) 26.

[7] Hill, *Greek Words,* 50–3, 59, 76; e.g., Deut 7:8; Ps 136:24; Isa 43:1.

[8] Douglas J. Moo, *The Epistle to the Romans* (Grand Rapids, Mich.: Eerdmans, 1996) 229.

[9] "You shall put the mercy seat on the top of the ark" (Exod 25:21).

hilastērion designates the *place* of atonement,[10] and is the word used throughout the LXX for the mercy seat (and also in Heb 9:5). The *hilastērion* is the place where an expiation (cleansing), a ritual sprinkling, occurs, but it is not itself the expiatory or sacrificial victim. Bailey's dissertation proves this.

In Romans 3:25, then, we need first to recognize that Jesus is being metaphorically equated with the mercy seat. We can expand our interpretation if we have supporting data, but we must start there. Of course, the Yom Kippur purification offerings are the most important sacrificial rituals of the year. Because of this, and because of the mention of "blood," it is understandable that scholars have overinterpreted the passage to make Jesus into the sacrificial victim, when actually Paul equates him with the mercy seat. But such overinterpretation blocks a fresh understanding of what Paul really said.

There is a soteriological formula at the end of the next chapter that has no cultic associations. Paul's point in Romans 4 is the saving power of faith (4:13, 19-24). He insists that God reckoned Abraham to be just because of the latter's faith and *before* he was circumcised (4:9-12). Faith predates and outranks circumcision, then. Christians should practice faith, like Abraham did. Paul nails down the chapter with a soteriological formula: Jesus "was handed over to death for our trespasses and was raised for our justification" (4:25). The "for" prepositions have two different meanings here: he was killed for *(because of)* our sins and was raised for *(in order to bring about)* our resurrection. Without a doubt, then, the death of Jesus has a saving significance for Paul. It is like a new Yom Kippur ritual, and in other places will be compared to other rituals or events. In 4:25 there is no cultic metaphor, but the death was *due to* human sin, and was *designed to* bring about salvation.

I think it likely that Paul is comparing the death of Christ to a covenant sacrifice in Galatians 3:14, by which I do not mean the Mosaic covenant, but a common ancient ritual that accompanied a peace treaty between individuals or tribes.[11] Paul is emphasizing the social effect (extension of the blessing to Gentiles), not the cultic pattern, but it is possible that the cultic pattern is present, although it is much more obvious in other passages in Paul.

---

[10] Daniel P. Bailey, "Jesus as the Mercy Seat: The Semantics and Theology of Paul's Use of *Hilastērion* in Romans 3:25" (Ph.D. dissertation, Cambridge University, 1999) ch. 2 sec. 2, pp. 17–20; ch. 3, §4.3.5.1–3, 57–66; ch. 4, §3.3, 89–90; Appendix B, Note C, 248.

[11] The form of this ritual, overlaid with much narrative, can be discerned in Gen 15:8-21; Jer 34:18-20.

2.2 Scapegoat and New Creation in 2 Corinthians 5:21

At the end of a passage that contains some of Paul's most striking statements about God's love and the apostle's ministry of reconciliation comes a vivid but peculiar soteriological statement:

> For our sake he made him to be sin who knew no sin, so that in him we might become the righteousness of God. (2 Cor 5:21)

This idea of a sinless one *becoming* sin and a sinful community *becoming* righteousness is a scapegoat metaphor.[12] At the heart of the scapegoat ritual is an exchange of conditions: the pure goat takes on the community's sin, and the community takes on the goat's purity. This interchange is at the heart of Paul's soteriology. It is a *ritual* exchange: the community's ill is ritually transferred to the victim, and community well-being is the result. Morna Hooker has highlighted the interesting term "interchange" to describe Paul's soteriology,[13] but she neglects to mention that this interchange has a cultic basis. Ignoring the cultic background of Paul's metaphors is a spiritualizing strategy that enables some interesting, but ultimately unsatisfying, analysis. The enigmas in Paul's teaching will irritate and haunt the reader who does not take a look at the rituals that were so important to the common people in Paul's time and that provide the logic behind his metaphors. This one has the "strange mechanism of reversal"[14] characteristic of expulsion rituals. Paul perpetuates and spiritualizes the logic of cult practice.

As was discussed in the previous chapter, the interchange and expulsion pattern also takes place in the Greek *pharmakos* ritual where human scapegoats are selected, consecrated, have disease, sin, or curse transferred onto them, and are banished. It is likely that this rite had become rare by Paul's time, but it had been so memorialized in literature and tradition that it was a readily recognizable image.

What happens in 2 Corinthians 5:21 is like what happens in a reversal ritual, not like what happens in a law court. This passage does not describe "justification" but change of status, a new "becoming." Christ *becomes* sin, and people *become the righteousness of God*—a stunning reversal that has nothing to do with acquittal but everything to do with what happens when an animal or a person "becomes" sin and is

---

[12] McLean, *Cursed Christ*, 110–2; Dunn, *Theology*, 217.

[13] Morna D. Hooker, "Interchange in Christ," *JTS* n.s. 22 (1971) 352, 355.

[14] Burkert, *Structure and History*, 63.

banished by the community. Nor does a sacrificial victim undergo such a shameful *be-sinning*; it remains pure and can be brought into the Lord's presence. It is the expulsion victim that becomes impure after a sin-transfer and must be harshly and hastily banished.

The difference between sacrifice and scapegoat is not spelled out by Paul whose interest is not scholarly but soteriological. For him, both sacrifice and scapegoat (as well as redemption payment) are useful as metaphors for describing Christ securing salvation on the cross. Paul blends and commingles his different metaphors, picturing Christ as the antitype, the fulfillment of everything that people believed about purification rituals, redemption purchase, and sin-banishment, with the end result, for believers, not only of acquittal in the divine court, but the receipt of Godly character, *becoming* righteousness! Paul blends Level Four and Level Six Spiritualization: metaphorical redefinition of cultic concepts and a moral and spiritual transformation of persons.

Paul appropriates the notion of cultic exchange, then fills it with spiritual content. This is probably Paul's most effective transformation metaphor, especially if read in its context, as the culmination of a discussion of "groaning" while living in a physical body, yearning for the heavenly one (2 Cor 5:2-4), anticipating Judgment Day yet eager to proclaim the love of Christ (5:10-14), who died for all (v. 15), offering new creation, reconciliation (vv. 17-19), and undergoing a reversal ritual so that people can become the righteousness of God (v. 21).

The perceptive reader understood that Paul was describing the death of Christ in terms of cult. "Trespasses" are "not counted against" people (5:19) *because* they have been imposed on a ritual victim. One must recognize one's own death in *that* death: "one has died for all; therefore all have died" (2 Cor 5:14). Or perhaps it is recognizing a *debt*: we owed a debt; someone paid it for us; now we owe *that* person. Restated, with the cultic aspect inserted, we get this: salvation required a victim; Christ became the victim so that people might live; people now must live "for him who died and was raised for them" (v. 15). Notice how the debt and the cultic solution are assumed at the beginning. Salvation, apparently, could not be gained any other way. Paul speaks of God's kindness and eagerness to save, yet the *means* of salvation had to involve some kind of exchange, either cultic (sacrificial or scapegoat) or economic (redemption payment). Paul's arguments are not consistent with his metaphors; his arguments always defend the generosity and free will of God, but his metaphors imply that a transactional payment or ritual was necessary. There is a contradiction between a free gift and a necessary payment, but neither Paul nor most theologians have been willing to acknowledge that there is a contradiction here.

God makes us righteous by carrying out an expulsion ritual on the Messiah. Apparently, God's generosity could only be manifested through a ritual pattern; even God could not do it without following the necessary procedure. Assumptions about what God "could not do" lurk in the background of all atonement theories: God *could not* forgive unless God's offended honor were vindicated (Anselm), unless a sufficiently valuable and pure sacrifice were offered (Gregory the Great). Those authors will be covered in the next chapter, but Paul also has his assumptions. He seems to assume that some cultic pattern, like the scapegoat mechanism, was already in existence when God resolved to save. This perpetuates the notion that ritual patterns are themselves divine or emanate from the divine level. And it guarantees that ancient beliefs will reappear within the new belief. Sacrificial soteriology is spiritualized ritual rectification, appealing to people raised in cultic religions and experiencing distress about their spiritual status.

2.3 The Currency of the Curse in Galatians 3:13

2.3.1 Redemption and Curse

In Galatians 3:13 ("Christ redeemed us from the curse of the law by becoming a curse for us"), redemption and curse-transmission are blended. First, salvation is pictured as a ransom payment or a manumission payment, indicated by *exagorazō* ("redeem"). Elsewhere, he uses the unprefixed version of this verb, *agorazō*, to tell believers, "you were bought with a price" (1 Cor 6:20 and 7:23). These verbs, meaning "to buy,"[15] are often used to refer to the purchase of slaves.[16] Paul is saying that Christ's death "paid for" the captives of law, the slaves of sin, and that Christ took over their ownership. The image of costly payment is important to Paul. Some scholars argue that the notion of "buying" a people only summons up one image: Yahweh "obtaining" Israel by rescuing them from Egypt, but this argument (at least if rigidly argued) is weak because the Septuagint does not use *(ex)agorazō*

---

[15] McLean, *Cursed Christ*, 127; Archibald Robertson, *A Critical and Exegetical Commentary on the First Epistle of St. Paul to the Corinthians.* ICC (Edinburgh: T & T Clark, 1911) 129.

[16] Dale Martin, *Slavery as Salvation: The Metaphor of Slavery in Pauline Christianity* (New Haven: Yale, 1990) 63.

to describe that action.[17] If Paul wanted to make an Exodus reference clear, he would have done better to choose from the "ransoming" verbs, *lytroō* and its related verbs. Instead, he seems deliberately to be heightening the metaphor of *purchasing* with his choice of *agorazō* verbs, with marketplace connotations. It is entirely possible that Paul uses a general purpose "purchase" verb so that Gentiles in his audience can hear a slave-freeing metaphor, while Jews can perceive the image of God obtaining a people.

Paul links his purchase metaphor with a scapegoat image. *Becoming a curse* is an "emphatic"[18] or "metonymic"[19] way to speak of being cursed or bearing a curse, a literary way of saying the curse is *transmitted* to the victim. Curse-transmission is one of the key moments in expulsion rituals, and seems to be Paul's particular focus in Galatians 3:13 and 2 Corinthians 5:21. The biblical scapegoat also is described as accursed in early Christian teaching[20] and in Jewish sources.[21] Sacrifices do not become accursed.

Observe how thoroughly Paul blends the purchase and scapegoat metaphors in Galatians 3:13. He makes the cultic act the *currency* that pays the ransom: Christ redeems *by* becoming a curse. The scapegoat exchange somehow *pays the ransom*. The judicial element is also present, since condemnation is entailed in Galatians 3:10 (the result of disobedience), and justification is the question in 3:11. However, the climactic moment concerns not Christ's *judicial* status but his *ritual* status (becoming a curse). He takes on a negative *ritual* condition so that humanity can take on positive *judicial* and *social* conditions (acquitted and freed).

So the threefold metaphor in Galatians 3:10-13 is this: Christ takes away our curse by becoming a scapegoat, purchases the freedom of the captives of sin, and secures a favorable judicial result for human plaintiffs in the divine court. His death bore away sin, paid a redemption price, and sprang the accused. Paul is deliberately blending these

---

[17] Lyonnet admits the latter point, but still argues for an Exodus reference ("Terminology," 114–5).

[18] McLean, *Cursed Christ*, 124.

[19] Kjell Arne Morland, *The Rhetoric of Curse in Galatians: Paul Confronts Another Gospel* (Atlanta: Scholars, 1995) 71. An example is: "I will make them . . . to be a curse" (Jer 29:18 [NAB]); cf. Morland, 256.

[20] *Barnabas* 7:7, 9; Tertullian, *Adv. Marc.* 3.7.7; Stökl Ben Ezra, *Impact of Yom Kippur,* 152–8; Grabbe, "Scapegoat," 162; McLean, *Cursed Christ,* 83–4.

[21] Philo, *Spec. Leg.* 1.188 (McLean, *Cursed Christ*, 82–3); and implied in *m. Yoma* 6:4 (Stökl, *Impact*, 159).

metaphors so that sin riddance (originally ritual) may take on judicial and social meaning. The cultic metaphor conveys solemnity and holiness; the redemption metaphor communicates costliness; the judicial image is hardly a metaphor, since Paul knows there will be a Judgment Day, with acquittals and convictions. But the others may not be metaphors either, in Paul's mind, if Christ is the *final* sacrifice, the *full* redemption, that all previous transactions only anticipated.

But salvation is not cost-free for the believer who must be willing to "suffer with him" (Rom 8:17). Co-suffering and even co-death (at least a symbolic death) are necessary parts of being connected to the Messiah who suffers. Being "united with him in a death like his" (Rom 6:5) refers mainly to "dying" to one's selfish desires. Whoever recognizes the Messiahship[22] of Jesus and the significance of his death becomes attached to the Messiah, takes on his righteous character, and will be raised from the dead as he was—and as Abraham was, too: Abraham was able to become a father, even though his old body "was as good as dead" (Rom 4:19). Salvation always takes this pattern of dying and being raised from the dead. But it all emanates from that first resurrection—the Messiah's. Christ's death and resurrection achieves a redemption that no one else's has to achieve.

2.3.2 Covenants and Curses

Some scholars wish to place the curse of Galatians 3:13 firmly within the framework of Deuteronomistic theology.[23] Indeed, Paul quotes Deuteronomy 27:26 and 21:23 (as well as Lev 18:5) in Galatians 3:10-13. The curse referred to twice in Galatians 3:10 is the curse invoked against covenant breakers in Deuteronomy. But the third occurrence, in Galatians 3:13, is not from Deuteronomy, which make no provision for any entity rescuing someone else from a curse. The whole community can rescue itself if it repents (Deut 30:1-5), but the curse is not removed by *someone else*. Only in Levitical cult is there such a sudden transfer of the community's curse to a curse-bearer, such a magical reversal of conditions between the community and a victim. We cannot ask Paul to stick to a Deuteronomistic mindset when he

---

[22] *Christ* is Greek for *Messiah*, which is both Aramaic and Hebrew for "anointed one." Kings, priests, and prophets could be anointed in ancient Israel, so "Messiah" could imply the qualities of one or more of those offices.

[23] Morland, *Rhetoric of Curse*, 63, 71, 237–9, and throughout. "Deuteronomistic" includes literature beyond Deuteronomy itself, while "Deuteronomic" refers to Deuteronomy itself.

prefers blending that with the Levitical and prophetic mindsets, and even with the Hellenistic universalizing instinct. The "curse of the law" in Galatians 3:13 blends the Deuteronomic threat-curse with the Levitical curse that can be carried away; the solution is Levitical, a *ritual* rescue, not a repentance of the nation.

Deuteronomy simply is not sufficient to explain the imagery of Galatians 3 or any other soteriological formula in Paul. Paul's mission is inclusion of the Gentiles. The Deuteronomic covenant is a covenant with Israelites, for Israelites, and against Israelites (when they break it); it has nothing to do with Gentiles. Paul's covenant has everything to do with Gentiles: the purpose of Christ's deed is "in order that in Christ Jesus the blessing of Abraham might come to the Gentiles" (Gal 3:14), while in Deuteronomy the purpose of obedience is so that "the Lord will drive out all these nations before you" (11:23). Paul will quote Deuteronomy but never to promote Deuteronomy's nationalistic theology.

For Paul, Jesus is the Jewish Messiah, but he is also the World Messiah; he "died for all" (2 Cor 5:15; cf. Rom 5:18-19; 8:32), and it is through him, and through his message of "faith," that God's favor is universalized:

> Before faith came, we were imprisoned and guarded under the law until faith would be revealed. . . . In Christ Jesus you are all children of God through faith. . . . There is no longer Jew or Greek. (Gal 3:23, 26, 28)

Therefore, it is not likely that Galatians 3:13 is talking only about Jews being delivered from the Law; he is also saying that Gentiles are delivered from the danger of *becoming* subject to the Jewish Law.

God has set about to fulfill the promise to Abraham (Gen 12:3: "in you all the families of the earth shall be blessed") that Paul understands as a promise to "justify the Gentiles by faith" (Gal 3:8). The "inheritance" comes from that promise to Abraham, not from the later covenant with Moses (3:17-18). The test for membership in Abraham's family is not Israelite ancestry but belief in the Messiah: "Those who believe are the descendants of Abraham" (3:7).

Paul reinterprets the *sperma* ("seed," that is, offspring) promised to Abraham, traditionally understood to mean numerous descendants, as a singular descendant, the Messiah (Gal 3:16). Everything is keyed on the Messiah. Faith in the Messiah was always the key to receiving the promise (3:22), though this was obscured for a period when the Law acted as a disciplinarian (3:23-25). But now faith has come and can turn all races and genders and classes into children of God (3:26-28). It is the Messiah who enfolds the Gentile believers into Abraham's true lineage: "if you belong to Christ, then you are Abraham's offspring" (3:29).

I have said that Paul appropriates and spiritualizes Levitical cultic imagery. To some degree, he also spiritualizes the covenant of Deuteronomy, although for a different reason. Leviticus is a mine for soteriological imagery; Deuteronomy seems to provide some ideas for ecclesiology. Paul's warnings about irreverent behavior surrounding the Eucharist sound like the "blessing or curse" option placed before the Israelites in Deuteronomy, even including a threat of divine violence (1 Cor 11:27-32). It is likely that Paul's cultic ideas have a sociological parallel, that his notions of God responding to cult are parallel to his notions about salvation communicated through the rites of Eucharist and baptism, carried out in a social setting, with certain leaders conducting the ritual. But it would require another book to examine the connections between theology and church structure.

2.4 The Body of Sin in Romans 6 to 8

For Paul, salvation definitely means being saved *from* something: from sin, which is a demonic power that enslaves people (Rom 7:25), "deceives" and "kills" them (Rom 7:11). In fact, *nothing good* dwells in Paul's flesh (Rom 7:18); although he wants to do good, Paul is controlled by the sin within his body (7:19-20).

How is it that sin has so much power? It appears that sin pulled off a masterful trick: "Sinful passions, aroused by the law, were at work in our members to bear fruit for death" (Rom 7:5). Sin "seiz[ed] an opportunity in the commandment" (7:11)—most likely the commandment to be fruitful and multiply[24]—which let loose sexual desire, "working death in me through what was good" (7:13). "Those who are in the flesh cannot please God" (8:8). Paul's ascetic thinking and celibate practice, then, are inseparable from his soteriology, which is expressed in terms of being rescued from,

> the law of sin that dwells in my members. Wretched man that I am! Who will rescue me from this body of death? . . . I am a slave to the law of sin. (Rom 7:23-25)

[24] Boyarin, *Radical Jew,* 164–5, 169, 176–8; Frances Watson, *Paul, Judaism and the Gentiles: A Sociological Approach* (Cambridge: Cambridge University Press, 1986) 156.

He had given an answer a few sentences earlier: "you have died to the law through the body of Christ" (7:4). It is *Christ's* body, then, that rescues Paul and others from their sin-infected bodies. This rescue through a victimized *body* certainly looks like the scapegoat pattern. In Romans 6–8, *bodies* are controlled by the demonic power of sin (6:6, 12; 7:23; 8:10), but they are rescued through Christ's body (7:4; 8:3). The horror of being possessed and controlled by sin in one's own members, is relieved by a grand expulsion that also judges sin:

> For what the Law could not do, weak as it was through the flesh, God did: sending His own Son in the likeness[25] of sinful flesh and as an offering for sin,[26] He condemned sin in the flesh. (Rom 8:3 NASB)

Three principal metaphors are blended here: the judicial notion of condemnation *(katakrinō)*, the technical term for the purification sacrifice *(peri hamartias)*, and an implied scapegoat image (projecting all sin onto one body). Is sin convicted in court, is it cleansed by a sacrifice, or is it carried away by some flesh-creature? In this verse, it is done by all three! The "condemned flesh" is a judicialized scapegoat "for sin" (the literal meaning of *peri hamartias*).

Scapegoat logic seems also to underlie Romans 6:6: "our old self was crucified with him so that the body of sin might be destroyed, and we might no longer be enslaved to sin." Sin has been unloaded onto Christ's body, and is destroyed when Christ's body dies. He is blending the images of a sin-bearing scapegoat, a slain sacrificial animal, and a condemned sinner.

The believer must exercise some imagination to understand Paul's principle that the believer's own body of sin was crucified with Christ. Further, the believer must "put to death the deeds of the body" (8:13), which is surely some kind of ascetic instruction, although Paul (just as clearly) did not require celibacy for married persons (1 Cor 7:1-16). At the very least, it means a renunciation of sensualism. One's public acceptance of Paul's Gospel must have involved some kind of symbolic repudiation of the "old body of sin," perhaps embodied in the baptismal liturgy. Paul may not always have had to be very specific in his ascetic instructions; if people accepted that "the body is dead because of sin" (Rom 8:10) and that they must "crucif[y] the flesh with its

---

[25] "Likeness" in the sense of "form," not implying that the body merely *appeared* to be flesh.

[26] This preserves the sacrificial meaning of *peri hamartias*, "sin-offering" (Wright, *Climax*, 222).

passions" (Gal 5:24), they would take steps to repudiate their favorite sins. This difficult challenge is possible because one is a participant in Christ; one is really plugged into the Messiah and can replicate the deeds of the one who was able to fully reject sin's appeal.

Salvation involves a symbolic death for the believer: "we have been united with him in a death like his" (Rom 6:5). Since Christ died to sin, and "we have died with Christ" (Rom 6:8), we can recognize that our old "body of sin [was] destroyed" (6:6); people can cease to "set their minds on the things of the flesh . . . [which] is death" (8:5-6).

Thus are Paul's asceticism and his soteriology inseparable; one informs the other. Both *belief* and *action* are involved in experiencing salvation in a Pauline church. Simply describing this as "salvation by faith" is too abstract; it does not account for the life changes that would accompany membership in these communities.

The soteriology in Romans 8:3 is surrounded by an intense flesh-Spirit dualism in chapters 5–6 and in 8:5-9. The *exchange* in Romans 8:3, like that in 2 Corinthians 5:21 and Galatians 3:13, is pictured with a cultic metaphor. Christ is made a ritual victim, and then is vindicated. Christians are then enabled to fulfill "the just commandment of the law" (Rom 8:4). Then the Spirit who raised the Messiah will raise the Messiah's believer (Rom 8:11). Following the Messiah is how one follows God, and in the believer's personal experience, this means following the Spirit. It is "by the Spirit" that people put to death the fleshly body and by Spirit-leading that they become "children of God" (vv. 13-14). Elsewhere, Paul says that recognition of who the Messiah is makes one a child of God (Gal 3:26). Christ is simultaneously the final scapegoat, the price of redemption, the long-promised Messiah, the *reason* for God's fostering of Abraham's descendants, and the leader who teaches the children to live by God's Spirit. All these themes are crucial for Paul; none can be dropped out. Some readers evidently threw up their hands and said "there are some things in them [his letters] hard to understand" (2 Pet 3:16).

2.5 Summary of Paul's Expulsion Imagery

To the two passages (2 Cor 5:21 and Gal 3:13) that almost certainly use the scapegoat image for the death of Christ can be added three Romans passages (6:6; 7:4; 8:3) where there is a strong likelihood of expulsive imagery. The sin-bearing Son, the curse-carrying Christ, whose "body" acts as ritual victim, is one of Paul's central images, probably more prominent than the sacrificial imagery (but unfortunately not distinguished from sacrifice by many American and British scholars). In 1 Corinthians, he uses the *pharmakos* terms *perikatharmata* and *peripsēma* to describe the role of an apostle (4:13), and advises believers to "clean out the old leaven" (5:7)—to banish a sexual sinner. Expulsion is particularly suggestive to this apostle who is so sensitive to the presence of corruption in himself and in the world. Paul has a bluntly effective metaphor at hand in the scapegoat image. The sinful community changed places with Christ, and he, by dying, *banished* sin. To this are added vindication and resurrection, and more content can be added through the image of the heroic martyr (see next section).

The scapegoat image remained vivid and effective in the minds of subsequent Christians. The *Epistle of Barnabas*[27] and Tertullian[28] identify Christ with the accursed scapegoat, Justin Martyr says Christ was the Accursed One,[29] while the *Didache* either refers to being "saved by the Curse"[30] or to being "saved by the accursed it/him/herself."[31]

We have found that Paul utilizes several cultic metaphors to describe the effect of the Messiah's death: scapegoat (several times), the Passover lamb (1 Cor 5:7), the "place of atonement" cleansed during Yom Kippur (Rom 3:25), and possibly the covenant sacrifice that makes peace between tribes (Gal 3:14). He is not looking to harmonize these metaphors but to encapsulate the *significance* of the death. However, it must be noticed that in each of these cases it has a *ritual* significance. Salvation results from a cultic act.

If we add the redemption and acquittal metaphors to the cultic ones, we see that four different kinds of transactions are conflated (combined) by Paul to describe the saving effect of the death of the Messiah:

- *sacrificial:* salvation as a ritual cleansing resulting from the ceremonial devotion and killing of a victim;
- *scapegoat:* salvation as the ritual sending-away of sin;

---

[27] "His likeness to the goat . . . . the type of Jesus, who was destined to suffer" (*Barn.* 7:10).

[28] *Adv. Marc.* 3.7.7.

[29] *Dial. Trypho* 111.2; cf. 40.4; Nancy Pardee, "The Curse that Saves (*Didache* 16.5)," in *The Didache in Context: Essays on its Text, History and Transmission*, ed. C. Jefford. NovTSup 77 (Leiden: Brill, 1995) 175 n. 57.

[30] *Did.* 16:5 (trans. Maxwell Staniforth and Andrew Louth, *Early Christian Writings: The Apostolic Fathers* [London: Penguin, 1987] 198).

[31] Aaron Milavec, *The Didache: Text, Translation, Analysis, and Commentary* (Collegeville, Minn.: Liturgical Press, 2003) 83: "it" would refer back to the fiery testing *(pyrōsis)* mentioned nineteen words earlier.

- *judicial:* salvation as a writ of acquittal in the divine court;
- *monetary:* salvation as a purchasing of the freedom of captives or slaves.

Paul intertwines these images so thoroughly that Christians have ever since understood scapegoat as having judicial implications that it did not have in its original setting; have understood redemption as carrying sacrificial or scapegoat implications; have understood sacrifice as carrying weight on the day of final judgment. Christian discourse has so blended these ritual and ransoming images that they have long since ceased to be distinguished by most readers of the Bible. But we need to recognize what his original hearers undoubtedly knew, that he was blending different metaphors. We can then ask *what* the blending communicates. I think one thing is supersession, although this term is embarrassing to those who want to convince their Jewish friends that Christianity does not claim to supersede Judaism.

Paul's metaphors do imply that the old Yom Kippur and Passover have now been superseded. He implies that God works through cultic means, yet *this* cultic act supersedes the earlier ones. Christ is the end of the Law (Rom 10:4), fulfilling the Law and its rituals. He is the real scapegoat that the old scapegoat prefigured; he is the real *hilastērion*.

Christ now accomplishes what the cult was formerly thought to accomplish. Paul's innovations succeed because he gives a convincing spiritualized explanation of the "real" meaning of established religious symbols. Typology retains the connection with an old tradition while moving forward into new territory, mentally, spiritually, socially.

2.6 Hellenistic and "Noble Death" Motifs

To make the picture complete, we must observe also Paul's usage of Hellenistic philosophic concepts. Of course, Paul builds upon OT backgrounds and Messianic hopes but he also uses the teaching techniques of Hellenistic philosophers.[32] He treats the fellowships he founded as assemblies of his spiritual students in need of direction and nurture, recalling the attitude of Stoic,[33] Epicurean,[34] and Cynic[35] teachers.

---

[32] Abraham J. Malherbe, *Paul and the Popular Philosophers* (Minneapolis: Fortress, 1989) 68–77.

[33] Troels Engberg-Pedersen, *Paul and the Stoics* (Louisville, Ky.: Westminster John Knox, 2000) 102–10.

[34] Abraham J. Malherbe, *Paul and the Thessalonians: The Philosophic Tradition of Pastoral Care* (Philadelphia: Fortress, 1987) 68–71, 81–8.

[35] Malherbe, *Paul and Popular*, 5–7, 47–8, 72.

Paul writes in the letter genre as the Cynics did. Paul's impatience with religious zeal concerning food bears "an unmistakable affinity to the Cynic view that food as such is religiously indifferent,"[36] and his sayings about being slaves of sin bring to mind such Cynic sayings as, "evil alone makes one a slave; virtue alone frees. . . . You yourselves are slaves on account of your desire."[37]

Of course, the Jewish backgrounds are crucial, but Gentile backgrounds are also important when studying the "apostle to the Gentiles" (Rom 11:13), who was often understand by others in terms of Hellenistic philosophy.[38] Paul's familiarity with different belief systems is broad, and he makes effective reference to meanings recognizable by different groups. Paul cannot be comprehended unless his dual audience (Gentile and Jewish) is kept in mind.

Paul's idea of Christ dying for others recalls a major theme of Classical and Hellenistic literature called the "noble death" or "effective death." The glorification of self-sacrificing heroes communicates values of civic loyalty, heroism, and piety. Even as far back as Pindar, dying for the Greek fatherland is called a "holy sacrifice."[39] But the idea receives its classic formulation at the hands of the great tragedians Sophocles and Euripides. In Sophocles, heroes die for their friends, their city, or (in *Antigone*) for a religious principle.

Self-sacrifice is a frequent theme in Euripides' plays.[40] These noble deaths are described with great dramatic force. The chorus in Euripides' *Iphigenia at Aulis* declares: "She goes to stain with the drops of flowing blood the altar of the divine goddess and her own throat, her body's lovely throat."[41] Iphigenia dies for Greece: "I give my body to Hellas. Sacrifice me. . . . Lead me to the altar to sacrifice."[42] Sometimes

---

[36] Peter J. Tomson, *Paul and the Jewish Law: Halakha in the Letters of the Apostle to the Gentiles* (Minneapolis: Fortress Press, 1990) 248; cf. 273, 275.

[37] Heraclitus *Epistle 9*, 32–5 (Worley); *The Cynic Epistles: A Study Edition*, ed. A. Malherbe, SBLSBS 12 (Missoula, Mont.: Scholars, 1979) 213.

[38] Malherbe, *Paul and Popular*, 76–7.

[39] *Fragment* 78; Jeffrey Gibson, "Paul's 'Dying Formula': Prolegomena to an Understanding of Its Import and Significance," (Paper at SBL Annual Meeting, November 25, 2002) 7.

[40] Williams, *Jesus' Death*, 153–60; Jan Willem Van Henten and Friedrich Avemarie, eds., *Martyrdom and Noble Death: Selected Texts from Graeco-Roman, Jewish and Christian Antiquity* (London and New York: Routledge, 2002) 15–6, 31–3.

[41] *Iph. aul.*, lines 1515–17; from *Ten Plays by Euripides*, trans. Moses Hadas and John McLean (New York: Bantam Books, 1960) 351.

[42] *Iph. aul.* 1397–98, 1555; from Hadas and McLean, *Ten Plays*, 348, 352.

self-sacrifice is purely metaphorical, sometimes it is given a ritual setting, as happens with Iphigenia.[43]

In Plato, ethical and political principle motivates the noble death of
Socrates—it is out of loyalty to the laws of the city.[44] He will not be se-
creted out of jail because that would circumvent the laws of the city.

The language of "dying for" one's people or one's cause became familiar to the ears of everyone in the Hellenistic world, being a respected literary and philosophical concept. The rhetoric of noble death
enters into Hellenistic civic cults, courtroom arguments,[45] funerary
speeches,[46] and pep talks by soldiers.[47] Among the Romans especially,
it becomes a central theme in military and political rhetoric. Roman
soldiers could devote themselves to the gods of the underworld when
they knew they were going to die in battle.[48]

This theme (which we nowadays call "martyrdom") is adopted by
the Jews when they are faced with the necessity of dying for the Torah
during the repression of the Seleucid dictator, Antiochus Epiphanes IV,
who seeks to destroy Jewish religious practice in the second century
B.C.E. Second Maccabees and *Fourth Maccabees*[49] lionize some martyrs
who give their lives for the Torah at this time, saying that their deaths
vindicate the whole Jewish people (*4 Macc.* 17:10).[50] Martyr-deaths
have vicarious saving power.

In *4 Macc.* 6:29, the martyr Eleazar prays "make my blood their purification (*katharsion*[51]), and take my life in exchange (*antipsychon*) for
theirs." This notion of "blood" accomplishing purification and a successful substitutionary exchange is a sacrificial idea. The same three
concepts occur in *4 Macc.* 17:21-22: the land is *purified* and the martyrs
are, "as it were, a ransom (*antipsychon*) for the sin of our nation. And
through the blood of these devout ones and their atoning [*hilastēriou*]

---

[43] Gibson, "Dying Formula," 9.

[44] Plato, *Crito* 50B–51E, 52D; it flows directly from the argument for *doing right* in
49C–50A.

[45] Gibson, "Dying Formula," 11–6.

[46] Van Henten and Avemarie, *Martyrdom and Noble*, 16–8.

[47] Gibson, "Dying Formula," 16–20.

[48] Jan Willem Van Henten, *The Maccabean Martyrs as Saviours of the Jewish People: A
Study of 2 and 4 Maccabees.* JSJ Sup 57 (Leiden: Brill, 1997) 147; Van Henten and Avemarie,
Martyrdom and Noble, 19.

[49] This book is italicized because it is not in the Bible; Second Maccabees is in the
Catholic Bible.

[50] Van Henten, *Maccabean Martyrs*, 121.

[51] This later becomes a common term for martyrs in Christian literature (David A.
deSilva, *4 Maccabees* [Sheffield: Sheffield Academic, 1998] 149–50).

death,"[52] Israel is saved. This passage has often been compared to Romans 3's death as redemption and place of atonement.[53] In both Romans and *Fourth Maccabees*, the "blood" of martyrs accomplishes purification and atonement (with a *hilastēr*-word).

We are reading Hellenistic martyrdom language when we read, in Paul, of Christ dying "for us" or for "weak believers" (Rom 5:8; 1 Thess 5:10; 1 Cor 8:11). It is a small alteration to speak of dying "for our sins" (1 Cor 15:3; Rom 4:25; Gal 1:4). While focused on universal rather than national salvation, these passages do echo the "noble death" theme in Greek and Maccabean literature. Martyr-related themes in Paul include vicarious effect (the death rescues others), grateful recognition of such rescue, the martyr taking on the community's sin or curse, and shame that one's sin made such a sacrifice necessary (2 Cor 5:15; Gal 1:4). Of course, Paul's martyrology affirms a certain ideological identity but not a racial or cultural one. Lacking a genetic identity, Christians were an anomaly in the ancient world.

2.7 Cultic and Social Metaphors

Some scholars downplay or ignore Paul's language of Christ as curse, as Paschal Lamb, as Redeemer, in order to heighten the Hellenistic/Maccabean theme of noble death.[54] I find that Paul uses many metaphors as well as the martyr motif and even uses one metaphor to interpret another. The metaphors interpenetrate, yet they can be discerned as discrete building blocks that are differently combined in different passages. Paul has not invested everything in any one metaphor but he *has* invested everything in the *range* of metaphors, explaining the death of Christ as a saving event that accomplishes cleansing or freedom-purchase or establishment of a family-like community.

Martyrdom is not an alternative but an additive to the mix of metaphors for the effective death of Jesus. "He died as a martyr" does not transfer information from another realm; martyrs are, by definition, people who die for a cause. "He died as a Passover lamb" moves the

---

[52] At the end, I depart from NRSV. "Atoning death" is better than NRSV's "death as an atoning sacrifice."

[53] That there is an overlap of terms and ideas is undeniable, but Jan Willem Van Henten argues too hard that faith, blood, and *hilastērion* constitute a known *formula* ("The Tradition-Historical Background of Rom 3:25: A Search for Pagan and Jewish Parallels," in *From Jesus to John: Essays on Jesus and New Testament Christology in Honour of Marinus de Jonge*, ed. Martinus C. De Boer. JSNT Sup 84 [Sheffield: JSOT, 1993] 126).

[54] Such as Cilliers Breytenbach, Stanley Stowers, and David Seeley.

usual meaning of that term to another realm, the realm of a *human* death. Usages that make such an imaginative *transfer* of meaning from another realm can be called "metaphors." Martyrdom is not a metaphor, though it *is* an interpretive model.

The martyrdom model can be mixed with the metaphors or left by itself. Many of Paul's references to Jesus' death are not spelled out; he simply says Christ died "for us" (1 Thess 5:10; 1 Cor 15:3), and this will probably evoke the concept of the noble death, a death that rescues others or rescues a whole community. But there is something more than just a rescue of friends in such a passage as Romans 4:25; Christ was put to death "for our trespasses," seeming to imply the sins of the whole human race. Rectifying all sin goes beyond what was ever claimed in previous martyrological literature. Christian interpretation has always understood Christ as a martyr and much more than a martyr. The various metaphors say more than does the martyrdom model regarding how humanity's relationship to God was changed.

Paul uses social metaphors to describe the beneficial *results* of Christ's death for believers: justification (a judicial metaphor), reconciliation (diplomatic), and adoption (familial, relational). Paul generally uses the martyr model and cultic and purchase metaphors for the saving transaction and social metaphors for the resulting new status of believers. The Messiah's sacrificial or scapegoat death suffices to bring about status-changing results for humans: acquittal, reconciliation, re-identification as children of God. Redemption can function in both halves of the saving formula: the *act* of redeeming is a metaphor for the saving death, but the reception of liberation is one of the beneficial aftereffects. So, people get a new status: innocent (when they had been guilty), reconciled (where they had been estranged), adopted as heirs (who formerly were mere servants), freed or redeemed (when they had been captives).

Current interpreters of Paul often highlight the concept of reconciliation, and this goes along with the etymology of our English word "atonement" meaning "making one" or restoring right relations. But the Hebrew and Greek atonement words mean expiating (cleansing) something or propitiating (appeasing) someone. Paul does use Greek words for reconciliation, but mainly just in two chapters (Romans 5 and 2 Corinthians 5), or three, if we include Colossians 1.[55] When Christians say "atonement" now, they mean several different things,

---

[55] Though no longer an "undisputed letter" of Paul, there is good reason to keep Colossians very close to Paul in terms of time and influence. Coauthorship is attributed to Paul and Timothy in 1:1.

derived from various metaphors found in Paul's and other letters of the NT (see next chapter).

Paul is able to make major alterations in the Jewish tradition by claiming to show the real meaning of the tradition. This is always the way of successful innovators: innovation is conveyed through traditional terminology and symbols, with arguments of continuity and fulfillment. Through reinterpretation, the OT remains valuable and can be retained, but nothing has the meaning it formerly had. Inheriting a land is turned into inheriting citizenship in a heavenly kingdom. The Mosaic "glory" is "fading" (2 Cor 3:7, 10), but it had really been pointing to the new glory all along. The OT narrative is seen to contain hidden meaning: "these things happened to them to serve as an example, and they were written down to instruct us" (1 Cor 10:11).

2.8 Pauline Soteriology

2.8.1 Explaining the Messiah to the Gentiles

How did it come about that the core message about salvation is an interpretation of the Crucifixion and Resurrection, while the teachings of Jesus himself became a secondary body of information? The shock and humiliation of the Messiah's death and the fact that only believers (and Paul!) experienced visitations from the risen Christ are part of the reason.

Since the Messiah was expected to be a Victor and Savior, but Jesus had died the death of a criminal, it became an urgent necessity to explain exactly *how* this Messiah was Victor and Savior, exactly *when* his judgment would prevail, and *where* his writ would run. These were explained with at least two very different schemes: *future eschatology*, with its promise of a Day of Judgment, and *typology*, which explains that certain crucial things have already happened: the Messiah has fulfilled the purpose of Yom Kippur and is even restarting the human race: he is a second Adam. What was of urgent interest for Paul was the identity of the Messiah and the significance of his death and resurrection rather than the content of his stories and maxims.

In the superheated field of debate about Israel, Messiah, and the Day of Judgment, Paul occupied the ideological position that eventually proved most persuasive among those Gentiles interested in the God of Israel. The content of his message highlighted the universal saving outreach of God, responding to every threat to that principle. He preserved the traditions about the God of Israel while yet explaining why circumcision and food laws do not apply to Gentiles. Paul chose a spiritualizing strategy that showed how the national cult pointed forward to a universal community. And he found a way to explain why the Gentiles poured into his churches while the majority of Jews were hardening their hearts to his message.

Paul was uniquely placed to affirm values from both the Jewish scriptures and the best of Gentile philosophy. He described the saving event in ritual, redemptive, and martyrological terms, while picturing its beneficial aftereffects in terms of status-improving Hellenistic institutions: acquittal, reconciliation, and adoption. He linked the martyrdom theme, so meaningful to Greeks and Romans, to Jewish monotheism. Gentile martyrology and Jewish piety are joined in the idea that "Christ died for the ungodly" (Rom 5:6).

2.8.2 What Does "Dying for Us" Mean?

One of Paul's repeated expressions is that Christ "died for us," by which he can mean—

he died to save us (martyr model)—

or: he died in our place (penal substitution model)—

or: he paid the price to buy our freedom (ransoming model)—

or: he died as the new place of atonement (sacrificial and typological)—

or: he took on our curse and bore away our sins (scapegoat, also typological).

In our day, as in Paul's, readers have their own patterns of "hearing" a mixture of these concepts. One reader takes it for granted that Paul is talking about a substitutionary death that "paid" a penalty. Another assumes that the emphasis is on heroic martyrdom, not on payment. A third sees the death of the innocent Messiah resulting in a cleansing overflow (combining ritual and moral ideas). It simply is not true that everyone hears the same thing in these formulas.

This conflation of concepts is understandable. Paul often uses one metaphor to interpret another. Believers were:

> justified [judicial]
>   by his blood [sacrificial or martyr image, or both] . . .
>   saved from the wrath of God [at Judgment Day] . . . .
>   were reconciled [social/diplomatic]
>   to God through the death of his Son [sacrifice and martyrdom].
>
> (Rom 5:9–10)

A cultic substance (blood) takes on monetary and judicial currency and social reconciling power. Do Christians today notice how elements from four different realms are here combined (not even counting the martyrdom model)? Do Christians really understand the complexity of doctrines and metaphors that are now labeled "atonement"?

Paul seems to be eager to combine several models for describing the death of Christ, each of which speaks of a transaction. The martyrdom or cultic death amounts to a redemption payment. The transactional nature of slave-redemption is conflated with sacrifice in its aspect of gift or payment to God. Martyrdom, too, is *holy* like a cultic act and also *worth* something in God's eyes (redeeming). Scapegoat joins the mixed image, bringing out the themes of transfer and expulsion of sin.

Even in the book of Acts we have a Pauline transactional metaphor. The author, Luke, understands Jesus as the long-promised Messiah vindicated by God, and situates the church story within a context of salvation history, but only *once* in Acts do any of his characters speak of blood-redemption, and that character is Paul, who says that the church was "obtained with the blood of his own Son" (Acts 20:28).

All these statements seem to imply that God is paid-off or persuaded, although Paul will not say this openly. But the logical implications of the metaphors say it, and the common people pick up on that. The metaphors imply a selfless Messiah, but a God who must be paid-off. Salvation is not free. Paul's various metaphors imply a *transaction* by which salvation is "bought with a price" (1 Cor 6:20).

This touches upon one of the difficulties in Paul: does he think that Christ's death changed God's mind, "purchasing" a salvation that otherwise would not have happened? Is salvation a result of God's generosity or of God being satisfied only after the required payment was made? Paul never says that God's mind was changed; in fact he says that *God* initiated the saving event (Rom 5:8), but the logic either of appeasement or of ritual cleansing shows up in the next verse where "his blood" turns away "the wrath of God" (Rom 5:9).

Again, in Galatians 4 he makes a sustained argument about the generosity of God, but still the actual salvation event was a transaction, "to redeem those who were under the law," mentioned only in passing in verse 5. So the answer seems to be yes and no; no, God was not persuaded (if you listen to Paul's longer, sustained arguments); yes, God was persuaded (if you look at the logic of the redemption and sacrifice metaphors).

But if it is the death itself that brought about salvation, what role does the exercise of *faith* play for the person seeking salvation?

2.8.3 Your Faith Has Saved You?

Both Jesus and Paul taught salvation by faith, leading to spiritual rebirth and alliance with God's purposes.[56] But while these were, for Jesus, freely available from the God who knows how to give his children what they need (Matt 5:6; 7:7-11), with Paul, salvation had to be *arranged*: there was a *mechanism* of salvation. Christ had to be *made* sin, had to be *handed over* for our transgressions. For Jesus, faith is primarily *trust*. This is present in Paul, but what dominates is an intellectual component, namely *belief*—assenting to certain soteriological facts: "Believe in your heart that God raised him from the dead" (Rom 10:9); "become obedient from the heart to the form of teaching to which you were entrusted" (Rom 6:17).

Faith, then, means accepting certain meanings of the Messiah's death and resurrection. Salvation does not come from Jesus' own teaching and ministry but from accepting soteriological formulas about the death of Jesus. For Paul, Christ is a *mediator*, not a proclaimer, of salvation. Jesus' own emphatically stated parables about faith, honesty, and growth may be fine wisdom teaching, but they are hardly the essence of salvation for Paul, which is "Christ, and him crucified" (1 Cor 2:2). A proclaimer of salvation is an apostle, and he never calls Jesus an apostle. For Paul, one dies to the Law not through the *teachings* but through the *body* of Christ (Rom 7:4). And so Jesus the teacher becomes Jesus the *type*, and a type needs to be interpreted.

Paul never says "your faith has saved you," as Jesus did,[57] since he is sure it was the Messiah's ultra-significant death that actually saves; rather, faith means accepting this teaching. Faith is saving not because it opens up communication with God, but because it attaches us to Christ who "attained access to this grace" (Rom 5:2) *through* his death, which "reconciled [us] to God" (5:10). Paul could never say "blessed are the pure in heart, for they will see God" (Matt 5:8), for there *are* no pure in heart in Paul's view. There is no immediate and free access to God by the meek or the pure. Access to God required an intervening transaction on behalf of wretched humanity: "Christ died for our sins" (1 Cor 15:3). Faith needs to believe *that*.

[56] Mark 3:35; Luke 7:50; John 3:3-8; Gal 3:26–4:6; Rom 12:2; Phil 3:9; Col 1:9.
[57] Luke 7:50; 8:48; 17:19; 18:42; Mark 5:34; 10:52.

Jesus was willing to use the innocence of children as a sign of the kingdom. For Paul, there is none innocent, and *trust* itself is not to be trusted since "the evil I do not want is what I do" (Rom 7:19). Paul's is a religion of catastrophic conversion;[58] Jesus' healthy-minded religion[59] is not understood. For Paul, there are only extremes: profound enslavement or unexpected redemption, being lost in sin or being dramatically rescued. And this experience is replicated in doctrines of a violent and sudden restoration of damaged relations with God.

Can we account for Paul's pessimism by saying that he is sensitive to the ever-present danger of human pride and sin? Is Paul, perhaps, more savvy to human deceptiveness than is Jesus, and never speaks of open and free access to God by the pure in heart because most people will dishonestly convince themselves that they are pure? Undoubtedly, Paul is perceptive on this point, but one can hardly say that he is more perceptive than Jesus, who could sniff out any scent of hypocrisy, or that Jesus' Gospel is the result of naivety. We are dealing with two entirely different instincts about God and access to God. Jesus, with fully adult know-how and lack of illusions, is able to say that a sincere and childlike faith opens the portals of heaven. There really *are* some truth-hungering, merciful, and "utterly sincere" people,[60] who "will be filled . . . . will receive mercy . . . . will see God" (Matt 5:6-8).

There is no denying that Paul's approach is a practical success. He seizes upon the most effective images that have deep resonance for the people of his day and for centuries thereafter, blending the ancient psychology of atonement with the new Gospel through a spiritualizing interpretation. But the open-hearted message of faith and sincerity that is clearly Jesus' central teaching (seen also in the parables and in the trust-recommending sermons of John 12–17) tends to be brushed aside by intense emotions of repentance and yearning and the mental construct of affirming certain soteriological formulas.

Despite the worthy motives of Paul's spiritualizing project, we must recognize that his rhetorical use of substitutionary metaphors ended up perpetuating certain primitive concepts of God that Paul himself could see through, as is shown by his insistence that God was not

[58] "Paul . . . passed through the misery of the 'sick soul' to the peace of the 'twice born'" (Kirsopp Lake, *The Earlier Epistles of St. Paul: Their Motive and Origin.* 2nd ed. [London: Rivingtons, 1919] 432–3).

[59] William James's concept.

[60] Matt 5:8 in J. B. Phillips, *The Gospels Translated into Modern English* (New York: Macmillan, 1961) 8.

persuaded but *initiated* salvation (Rom 5:8). Paul was willing to utilize soteriological formulas that embodied propitiation and persuasion because they "worked" with the people. Winning converts was his all-consuming motive: "I have become all things to all people, that I might by all means save some" (1 Cor 9:22). In the interests of making the Gospel marketable, Paul poured the new wine into old conceptual forms, spiced with a dose of spiritualizing, and enlivened by the real spiritual experience that he and his fellows were having. But this means that some incompatible religious ideas were yoked together. Whatever could "preach" could stay; but this has caused confusion to later Christians.

This is the danger of atonement metaphors, however rhetorically effective they may be: they carry their baggage with them, and leave these bags like time bombs in the railway stations of our thinking, prepared to explode into manifestations of fear, suspicion, and scapegoating.

Although Paul never expounds upon God being appeased by the death of Christ, that *is* an implication of his metaphors, and later Christians have developed such notions, particularly in the form of Christ's bearing some kind of substitutionary punishment. "Law" and "condemnation" occur thirty times in Romans 7–8. Some kind of substitution takes place in Romans 8:3—the Son indwelt sinful flesh, and God then "condemned sin in the flesh." We can see where Calvin got his idea of Jesus' flesh becoming the focus of God's wrath. Even if this grossly exaggerates one aspect of Paul's teaching, it has a real basis in Paul's words. Paul cannot be blamed for the very literal-minded and morbid theologies that lesser minds have developed, but we also cannot deny that these theologies grew out of the Pauline tradition.

Most of the problems with atonement have some basis in biblical texts. Despite the efforts of many theologians to separate the objectionable from the biblical, the notions of appeasement and buyout do have a basis in Pauline and deutero-Pauline metaphors that pick up on the manipulative psychology of sacrifice and redemption. All this has no basis in Jesus' Father, who is eager to give the children what they need without having to be persuaded.

So, what *are* the concepts that postbiblical thinkers developed regarding salvation, trust, and the death of Jesus; and how have recent thinkers dealt with the disturbing implications of some formulations of atonement? These are the subjects of the next two chapters.

Atonement after Paul

3.1 Domesticating Paul

3.1.1 The Conservative Deutero-Pauline Tradition

Even in Paul's own lifetime, and certainly shortly thereafter, many people found it difficult to comprehend his concepts. In particular, his idea of participating in Christ's sufferings, thus enabling later participation in his resurrection, was apparently too mystical to be preserved. So also may have been the practice in his churches, that "you can all prophesy one by one" (1 Cor 14:31). His notion of high participation in the messianic pattern, even to the point of "completing what is lacking in Christ's afflictions" (Col 1:24), was more than the emerging authority structure in the church could tolerate. Instead, his successors simplified and domesticated Paul, toning down his radicalism and heightening his conservatism. This is clearly evident in the Pastoral Epistles (the Timothy letters and Titus), which most (not all) scholars consider to be pseudepigraphical: attributed to, but not written by, Paul.

The Pastorals are interested in preserving "sound doctrine" (Titus 1:9; 2:1; 2 Tim 4:3) or "sound teaching" (1 Tim 1:10; 4:6) that will silence the "idle talkers . . . the older men . . . . the older women" (Titus 1:10; 2:2-3) in the church, and refute certain "teachers" to whom those "having itching ears . . . will turn . . . and wander away" (2 Tim 4:3-4). Thus does Paul's actual teaching become less important than his usefulness as an authority figure who stands against any independent teaching. The figure of "Paul" is used as a mouthpiece for the teachings of bishops[1] who are trying to shut down certain alternative expressions dismissed as "teachings of demons . . . profane myths" (1 Tim 4:1, 7), "senseless controversies . . . . counterfeit faith" (2 Tim 2:23; 3:8), and "quarrels about the law" (Titus 3:9) that are succeeding

---

[1] Bishops, more literally *overseers*, are mentioned in 1 Tim 3:2; Titus 1:7. They are clearly authority figures, but not celibate "priests," in the Pastorals (see 1 Tim 3:2-15).

in drawing aside "silly women" (2 Tim 3:6), "busybodies" (1 Tim 5:13), and the "perverted and sinful" (Titus 3:11). Clearly, there is intense competition for the Pauline legacy, and the Pastorals represent the winning interpretation, the one that affirmed structured male leadership, simplified doctrine, self-control (but not excessive asceticism: 1 Tim 2:15; 4:3; 5:23), and strong in-group loyalty. The now-forgotten losers are called "liars" (1 Tim 4:2), "Cretans" and "liars" (Titus 1:12), and those "holding to the outward form of godliness but denying its power" (2 Tim 3:5).

The values in the Pastorals are conducive of social cohesion: modesty, silence, temperance, self-control (1 Tim 2:9-11; 3:2; Titus 1:8), "integrity, gravity, and sound speech" (Titus 2:7-8). Everyone must stay in his or her social sphere and not agitate: "young women . . . being submissive to their husbands. . . . Tell slaves to be submissive to their masters" (Titus 2:4, 5, 9). Strict sex roles are advanced: "I permit no woman to teach or to have authority over a man; she is to keep silent" (1 Tim 2:12). The overseer must be a man (1 Tim 3:4) "well thought of by outsiders" (3:7), and female behavior must "give the adversary no occasion to revile us" (5:14) and so reduce persecution—a choice for prudence in the intensely role-conscious and identity-conscious setting of the Roman Empire. This sounds like the conservatism of Paul in Romans 13, but it does not sound like the Paul who refers to a number of women coworkers, including the woman apostle Junia[2] in Romans 16:7.

3.1.2 Making Redemption Dominant

Looking at the Pastorals and at other deutero-Pauline literature, we see that Paul's metaphors get turned into doctrinal formulas, with sacrifice and redemption conjoined, justification subordinated, and scapegoat and adoption fading out. Paul's subtleties are lost on his successors who fuse together and freeze his metaphors. Redemption becomes the controlling figure. Even sacrifice is understood in terms of redemption:

> In him we have redemption through
> his blood. (Eph 1:7)[3]   *[redemption, sacrifice]*

---

[2] Dunn, *Theology*, 587.

[3] Ephesians seems to be a spin-off of Colossians. Most scholars consider it deutero-Pauline.

> Christ . . . gave himself a ransom
>   for all. (1 Tim 2:6)   *[martyrdom, ransom]*

> . . . who gave himself for us that he might redeem us from all iniquity
>   and purify for himself a people of his own.
>   (Titus 2:14)   *[martyrdom, redemption, purification]*

> You know that you were ransomed from the futile ways . . . with the
>   precious blood of Christ, like that of a lamb without defect or blemish.
>   (1 Pet 1:18-19)[4]   *[ransom, sacrifice]*

Penal substitution and death-as-payment are indissolubly blended and have been treated as one notion ever since.

The conflation of metaphors in the post-Pauline era is mainly directed toward solidifying Paul's rapidly shifting metaphorical stream, usually by making redemption-sacrifice dominant. The Epistle to the Hebrews takes another tack, making sacrifice the dominant image, with Christ being both high priest and sacrificial victim.

In Paul's own soteriology there is a strong suggestion of penal substitution, but it should not be so magnified as to obscure the other ingredients of the Pauline *exchange* (a sin-bearing that results in an exchange of curse for blessing, of sin for righteousness), nor to obscure the dimensions of *cosmic rescue* and *typological fulfillment*. Christ is martyr-rescuer, punishment-bearer, and promise-fulfiller. Typology conveys a strong sense of salvation history and fulfillment, emphasizing that God had always intended to save all humanity, not just Israel.

Jesus' role, then, for Paul, was heroic, tragic, and triumphant. Post-Pauline thought certainly has a tragic and triumphant soteriology but the humanly heroic function of Christ and the history-of-salvation depth of his mission disappear from view. In the Gentile church, it is taken for granted that Jesus would save Gentiles, but the interesting attempt to explain that in terms of salvation history fades out. The originality and sharpness of Pauline metaphor is replaced by increasingly predictable formulaic utterances by those whose main interest is to ensure that no one departs from "sound words" or "sound doctrine" (1 Tim 6:3; Titus 2:1).

This is not entirely alien to Paul; rather, it represents one side of his teaching, the side that wants people to "become obedient from the heart to the form of teaching to which you were entrusted" (Rom 6:17). Here, the believer is entrusted to a *teaching*, and to "righteousness"

---

[4] A letter combining Petrine and Pauline traditions, given final shape by someone with excellent Greek.

(v. 18). Paul, then, had opened the door to depicting salvation as loyalty to a teaching, and it is that conservative aspect of his teaching that
comes to dominate the church.

3.2 Development of the Doctrines of Atonement

A study of the key patristic[5] developers of the Christian doctrine of
atonement finds that they do something that Paul does (find saving
significance in the death of Jesus) but also do something that Paul
never does: locate the *full* significance of salvation in one particular
metaphor for the death as an atoning act. Paul switches metaphors
with a rapidity that suggests that any one metaphor, by itself, would
be misleading. Further, he is always looking ahead to the Resurrection,
and his understanding of atonement is never separated from his notion that dying with Christ foretells rising with Christ (due to Christ's
resurrection power). Theologians have tended to glue together Paul's
atonement metaphors into the notion of a sacrificial and redeeming
transaction that took place at the cross and that literally (not metaphorically) cleanses sin and pays the debt for human sinning.

J. Denny Weaver organizes the postbiblical doctrines of atonement
into the "Christus Victor" concepts (in which Christ is victorious over
the devil and his forces), the satisfaction theory (Christ paying or suffering a penalty that humanity owed or incurred), and the moral influence theory (Christ's heroic death can move people to repent and be
loyal).[6] The Christus Victor branch further subdivides into two, (a) the
ransom theory, in which the devil was tricked into thinking it had
gained power over the Son by killing him, but by raising him from the
dead, God triumphed over death and the devil, freeing the devil's captives; and (b) the "cosmic battle" version that stresses Christ's resurrection and his defeat of evil.[7] He is largely relying on Gustaf Aulén,
the scholar who revived attention to the Christus Victor understanding.[8] I organize them somewhat differently, but the reader will be able
to recognize the similarities.

---

[5] The church fathers and writers of the second to seventh centuries.

[6] J. Denny Weaver, *The Nonviolent Atonement* (Grand Rapids, Mich.: Eerdmans, 2001)
151–3.

[7] Ibid., 15.

[8] Gustaf Aulén, *Christus Victor: An Historical Study of the Three Main Types of the Idea of
the Atonement* (London: Society for Promoting Christian Knowledge, 1931) 23–8, de-
fending what he calls "the classic idea."

3.2.1 The Rescue Theories

I use this term to include both the Christus Victor and the so-called ransom theories. The first church father at whom I look certainly does speak of a ransom paid. But he and the others in this group do not emphasize payment so much as cosmic *rescue* and the triumph over evil forces, so I prefer to call these theories of the early Greek fathers, the rescue theories.

Irenaeus does allow that Christ's death was a ransom payment to the devil, but this notion is not developed[9] and does not form the core of his soteriology. For one thing, the devil had not gained his rights over humanity legitimately but by violence.[10] Irenaeus sees Christ rescuing humanity by rescuing human nature itself. This is known as the doctrine of "recapitulation." Christ restores each progressive phase of human life by living through it; his obedience in each stage of life repairs the damage done by human sin.[11] Irenaeus will repeat standard notions like "ransom," but they fit into a larger framework: a *soteriology of repair*, with Christ as second Adam of a restored human race, capable once again of imitating God.[12]

The systematic theologian Origen of Alexandria sees the whole life and teaching of Christ as saving.[13] This really follows a completely different logic than any of the concepts of atonement. But Origen has no problem using models that operate on completely different kinds of logic. He accepts most of the ideas of his predecessors: a ransom paid to the devil, innocent blood having expiatory value, and dying in the place of sinners.[14] He also says the ransom payment was really a deception since God knew the devil could not maintain control over a sinless soul.[15] But it seems that his dominant idea is the defeat of the devil and the evil spirits. I sometimes think of this as Star Wars soteriology: a great cosmic battle. Christ defeated the devil by rising from

---

[9] *Adv. Haer.* 5.1.1; Adolf von Harnack, *History of Dogma*, trans. Neil Buchanan (New York: Dover, 1961 [1900]) II:290.

[10] Bartlett, *Cross Purposes*, 63; Aulén, *Christus Victor*, 43; Harnack, *History of Dogma*, II:290.

[11] *Adv. Haer.* 2.22.4; 3.16-23; 4.20 and 38; 5.16-21; see Harnack, *History of Dogma*, II:238–42; 272–3, 288–93; J.N.D. Kelly, *Early Christian Doctrines*, rev. ed. (New York: Harper & Row, 1978) 172–4.

[12] Harnack, *History of Dogma*, II:240–2.

[13] Hastings Rashdall, *The Idea of the Atonement in Christian Theology* (London: Macmillan, 1919) 258.

[14] Harnack, *History of Dogma*, II:367.

[15] *Exhort. ad mart.* 12; *In Matth.* 16.8; 12.28; Harnack, *History of Dogma*, II:367.

the dead and freeing the spirits in prison (1 Pet 3:19) in the devil's realm.[16] The Resurrection is at the center of this theology. Christ and his Resurrection are life-giving fountains from which salvation springs. Justification means believers are really made righteous by Christ, not just acquitted because of him.[17] It goes even beyond this: Christians can be transformed into the likeness of Christ.[18] Human nature can now be divinized because God, in Jesus, came into human nature.[19] It is the Incarnation of the divine Son that enables and empowers ordinary people to allow the Spirit to be incarnated in their lives. Since the late fourth century, this concept has been known as *theōsis*,[20] and it is a logical outgrowth of incarnational theology. The Incarnation, the essential and unique doctrine of Christianity, need not be linked with atonement theology. In different church fathers, incarnational theology leans toward atonement or toward *theōsis* in different degrees.

A principal example of one who leaned toward *theōsis* (though he also retained atonement) was Athanasius, bishop of Alexandria. The distinctive emphasis of Athanasius is that the Incarnation is the key to "the restoration of the human race to the divine life."[21] Salvation is a salvage and restoration job that emanates from the Incarnation itself. "Through this union of the immortal Son of God with our human nature, all men were clothed with incorruption."[22] There is a progressive work of *theopoiēsis*, the transformation of the corruptible to the status of the incorruptible,[23] which may even mean that human bodies will have "the quality of incorruptibility restored to them."[24] Christ conquered the corruptible nature every day of his life. He "restored the divine image in us."[25] Only the one who was the perfect Image of God could re-create humanity in that image.[26] The divine Son came into the

[16] Rashdall, *Idea of the Atonement*, 261.

[17] *Hom. on Jeremiah* 15.6; Rashdall, *Idea of the Atonement*, 273, 287.

[18] *Con. Celsus* 8.17; cf. 1.68; Kelly, *Early Christian*, 184.

[19] *Con. Celsus* 3.28; Kelly, *Early Christian*, 185.

[20] The term was coined by the brilliant church father Gregory of Nazianzus. It is not really a "doctrine," but a group of concepts about participation in, and taking on the character of, God.

[21] Harnack, *History of Dogma*, III:289–90.

[22] *De incarn.* 9; *On the Incarnation*, trans. by a Religious of C.S.M.V. (Crestwood, N.Y.: St. Vladimir's Seminary, 1998) 35.

[23] Harnack, *History of Dogma*, III:294.

[24] According to Rashdall's understanding (*Idea of Atonement*, 298).

[25] Kelly, *Early Christian*, 377.

[26] *De incarn.* 13; *On the Incarnation*, p. 41.

human place so as to enable humans to be divinized, to be transformed by and into the divine nature.[27] This is certainly not a ransom theory, but it could be called a rescue theory.

Gregory of Nyssa does have a ransom theory, but "rescue theory" is still a better label, as we will see. Gregory picks up on the ideas of Irenaeus, but says something the latter never did: that the devil has *legitimate* power over humans, since they had sold themselves into the devil's power. God has no right to just steal people away from the devil, but has every right to *buy back* these people.[28] This forces Gregory to take the notion of a ransom payment more literally than Irenaeus did, but he then departs from the logic of ransom, bringing in a theme of deception. The devil was fooled, just "as greedy fish" are tricked into swallowing the fishhook with the bait.[29] The devil did not realize he was allowing the Power of Life into his house of death. Salvation thus was not really the result of a transaction with the devil, but a masterful trick upon, and conquest of, the devil. It is the Resurrection that accomplished the triumph, and that sets the pattern for repair and reuniting of divided human nature: a Platonic idea Christianized.

Gregory's friend Gregory of Nazianzus turns out to be his greatest critic on atonement theory. Gregory of Nazianzus denies that there is a ransom payment at all, either to the devil or to God. The devil is a robber, and "how shameful that the robber should receive not only a ransom from God, but a ransom consisting of God Himself!"[30] while God would not want such a payment; God never held humanity prisoner in the first place.[31] Gregory of Nazianzus cannot abide either the idea of God dealing with the devil or being paid off in any way. Further, Paul never meant that Christ really *became* a curse, but that he was treated *as if* he were accursed. Gregory anticipates the so-called "moral influence theory" of later centuries by stressing that Christ could have saved us any way he chose, but that he wanted to inspire people to imitate his sympathy.[32]

3.2.2 Augustine and Gregory the Great

Theōsis can still be found in the Latin fathers, but its importance has faded. The Latin fathers are more well known for spelling out exactly

[27] *De incarn.* 54.
[28] Bartlett, *Cross Purposes*, 68; Gregory's *Or. Cat. Mag.* 22.
[29] Gregory *Or. Cat. Mag.* 24, Rashdall, *Idea of Atonement*, 305; Bartlett, *Cross Purposes*, 69.
[30] *Or.* 45.22; Kelly, *Early Christian*, 383.
[31] Rashdall, *Idea of Atonement*, 309.
[32] Ibid., 310.

what logic they see underlying the atonement transaction. Augustine is by far the most influential theologian writing in Latin. He restates the ransom/rescue theory: humanity is under the power of the devil, but God tricked the devil, enticing him like a mouse into a mousetrap.[33] Then Augustine introduces Roman legal terminology into the story: the devil overstepped his legal rights by attacking the divine Son and thereby lost his rights to "detain anyone who has put on Christ."[34] What Augustine's narrative shows is the ransom theory being replaced, mid-story, by a legal theory. First Christ is offered as a kind of ransom payment, but this turns out to be a trick, and when the devil attacks Christ, this triggers a *legal* penalty against him. Still, the death can be described as a sacrifice for sins or as a penal substitution: Christ suffered the "penalty owing to our sin."[35] It seems to be taken for granted that humanity as a whole can be condemned and that a legal remedy is needed. Legal theories dominate all the Latin theologians from Tertullian[36] to Augustine to Gregory the Great, reflecting a Roman intuition about the fundamental importance of law, even on the divine level.

Augustine is the formulator of the theory of original sin that became dominant in the Western tradition, with notions such as the sinfulness of all the offspring of sexual union, the damnation of babies due to their willful sinfulness,[37] and the "cruel necessity of sinning"[38] whereby people cannot help but sin. Since all people were hopelessly sinful, "a mediator (reconciliator) was necessary, who should appease this wrath (justa vindicta) by presenting a unique sacrifice."[39]

Pope Gregory the Great was the great popularizer of Augustine's ideas. Salvation takes on the pattern of the Roman idea of rewards and punishment, legal process, and the role of intercessors in court. Legal and sacrificial concepts are blended. Gregory argues that human sin made a human sacrifice necessary: First of all, man was a debtor because of his sin, and so allowed himself to be handed over to the devil's power.[40] For every sin there must be a penalty. As Dudden summarizes Gregory, there must be

---

[33] *Sermon* 263.1; Bartlett, *Cross Purposes*, 72; Kelly, *Early Christian*, 391.

[34] *De Trin.* 13.16; Bartlett, *Cross Purposes*, 72 n. 80; cf. Kelly, *Early Christian*, 392.

[35] *Enchir.* 41; *Enarr. in Ps.* 64.6; *C. Faust. Manich.* 14.7; Kelly, *Early Christian*, 392–3.

[36] An excellent account is found in Harnack, *History of Dogma*, V:16–20.

[37] *Faith, Hope and Charity* 8.27; Bartlett, *Cross Purposes*, 59–60.

[38] *De perfect. iustit. hom.* 4.9; Bartlett, *Cross Purposes*, 59.

[39] Harnack, *History of Dogma*, V:225, who is paraphrasing a passage in *Enchiridion Laur.* 33.

[40] Gregory's *Moral Teachings from Job* 17.47; 3.29; Dudden, *Gregory the Great*, 338, 340.

a proportionate sacrifice. But what sacrifice could man offer, which should be great enough . . . ? "It was not just," says Gregory, "that for rational man mere brute beasts should be sacrificed. . . . What was required, then, was a rational victim, that is, man; and a victim capable of cleansing, that is, sinless man."[41]

Gregory's logic compels him to say that only a human sacrifice—and only a *sinless* human—would suffice as payment. This is the most crude and literal—but fully logical—expression of the combined judicial/sacrificial atonement concept. There is an intense contrast between implacable Father and compassionate Son. The death of the Son "moderated the wrath of the Judge."[42] Bartlett says that, with Gregory the Great, "the scheme of divine violence is established," including the doctrine of punishment in purgatory.[43]

Gregory gives us some more morsels of atonement doctrine, doctrines that would dominate Christianity through the Dark Ages. He thought the Incarnation was a *necessary* trick, so that the devil would be willing to attack the Son and thus lose his rights over humanity. Satan was smart enough to know he should not attack the Son of God, but the humility and suffering of Christ made him think that Christ could not be that person.[44] The weakness of ransom theories is that they invite such notions, all of which see God as less than all powerful. The challenge to theology is to retain the full sovereignty, along with the full goodness, of God.

3.2.3 The Satisfaction Theory

All of this lays the groundwork for Anselm's *Cur Deus Homo?* which can be called "the master-text of divine violence,"[45] or "the emancipation of the Church from this hideous theory" of a ransom paid to the devil.[46]

In the eleventh century, Anselm constructs a theory based on the social structure of his time; he gives a "feudal structure" to salvation.[47]

---

[41] Dudden, *Gregory the Great*, 341; citing *Moral* 17.46; cf. 9.54.

[42] *Moral* 9.61; Dudden, *Gregory the Great*, 342.

[43] Bartlett, *Cross Purposes*, 74. A full appreciation of Bartlett's analysis cannot be had until we examine the theories of René Girard in the next chapter, in the section "Sacrifice as Sacred Violence."

[44] *Moral* 33.14; Dudden, *Gregory the Great*, 339.

[45] Bartlett, *Cross Purposes*, 76.

[46] Rashdall, *Idea of Atonement*, 350.

[47] Cynthia S. W. Crysdale, *Embracing Travail: Retrieving the Cross Today* (New York: Continuum, 1999) 112.

Society is used as an allegory, with God as a feudal lord and humanity as serfs.[48] The lord of the manor provides protection, the serfs work the land and always give honor to their lord. In this analogy, sin breaks the agreement since it dishonors God; sin is fundamentally an affront, and does damage to the lord's honor.[49] God, then, is like an offended Lord who cannot afford to let his servants show disrespect; there must be *satisfaction*, so God's honor may be restored.

Satisfaction is comparable to the payment of "civil damages,"[50] but usually by some form of compensation "other than by direct payment"; other forms of giving or of suffering (undergoing a mutilation, for instance) could make satisfaction.[51] Satisfaction is a structured form of vengeance,[52] then, a reparation for dishonoring someone. The death of Christ recompenses for the dishonor generated by human sin. Christ's innocence and his undeserved death earn a treasury of merit that suffices to pay off humanity's sin-debt.[53] It certainly looks like God has the same pride and status consciousness that an eleventh-century lord had. Jesus literally "pays" with his life a debt incurred by others.

Indeed, the devil is left out of the equation, but Bartlett says that Anselm's move only means that the source of violence against humanity is no longer the devil but God the Father. So "divine unity and sovereignty are saved but divine violence is established formally and metaphysically."[54]

Is this a fair restatement? David Hart and Daniel Bell think it is not, and they try to argue that Anselm's analogy transcends the economic and judicial spheres, revealing "an *aneconomic* order of charity, plenitude, and ceaseless generosity."[55] But this is not convincing. This "plenitude" is negotiable like wealth and is paid as a *satisfaction*; these are still *within* the economic and legal spheres. Feminists are right to point out that this is not a healing dynamic but reflects an honor/shame mentality: "Anselm's . . . view of justice is not that wrong should be

[48] Joel B. Green and Mark D. Baker, *Recovering the Scandal of the Cross: Atonement in New Testament and Contemporary Contexts* (Downers Grove, Ill.: IVP, 2000) 22.

[49] Timothy Gorringe, *God's Just Vengeance: Crime, Violence and the Rhetoric of Salvation* (Cambridge: Cambridge University Press, 1996) 93.

[50] Rashdall, *Idea of Atonement*, 351.

[51] Gorringe, *God's Just Vengeance*, 89.

[52] Ibid., 100–1.

[53] Rashdall, *Idea of Atonement*, 354.

[54] Bartlett, *Cross Purposes*, 66.

[55] Daniel M. Bell Jr., "Sacrifice and Suffering: Beyond Justice, Human Rights, and Capitalism," *Modern Theology* 18 (2002) 344, restating Hart's position.

righted but that wrongs should be punished . . . to pay back the honor."[56] God's *pride* is at stake—or is it the pride of a theologian who can only think in terms of the social structures of his own day?

Yet, even though Anselm describes sin as tarnishing God's honor, he can also say that it is impossible to tarnish God's honor. He has no problem uttering statements that come from two conflicting systems of logic: sin "disturbs the order and beauty of the universe . . . although he cannot injure nor tarnish the power and majesty of God."[57] Gunton and Peters claim that it is moral order, and not satisfaction, that is at the heart of Anselm's view of sin, and that Anselm should be commended for stressing the need for cosmic order.[58] But all of this order shows no fundamental departure from feudal order, and this morality differs not at all from retaliatory medieval justice. Further, even Gunton must admit that Anselm "seems . . . over-systematic in his exposition . . . . taking too literally the allusion to ransom . . . treating the blood as an actual price and asking whether it was paid to God or to the devil."[59]

It is best to frankly admit that Anselm's theory tries to fit God and humanity into a medieval framework. The crudeness of the attempt is obvious now that the framework has passed away, and this should serve as a warning to all theologians against imposing time-limited models of thinking upon the offer of salvation that has been made to the humans of all ages and cultures. Of course, there are elements of payment in Paul's teaching, and it suggests the purchase or manumission of slaves, an image from social structures of *Paul's* time. Still, that Paul intended his listeners to exercise some flexibility of imagination is shown by his continual mingling of metaphors; hopefully, no one metaphor would be taken too literally.

Weaver's criticism of the satisfaction theory is that it "lacks a role for resurrection in salvation, it is not apocalyptic in orientation, and therefore is incompatible with Paul."[60] To argue this, Weaver must evade the full force of Paul's focus on the saving significance of the

---

[56] Joanne Carlson Brown and Rebecca Parker, "For God So Loved the World?" in *Christianity, Patriarchy, and Abuse: A Feminist Critique,* ed. Joanne Carlson Brown and Carole R. Bohn (New York: Pilgrim, 1989) 7, referring to *Cur deus homo* 1.11-12.

[57] *Cur Deus Homo?* 1.15.209; Bartlett, *Cross Purposes,* 81.

[58] Colin E. Gunton, *The Actuality of Atonement: A Study of Metaphor, Rationality and the Christian Tradition* (Grand Rapids, Mich.: Eerdmans, 1989) 89–96; Ted Peters, "Atonement and the Final Scapegoat," in *PRSt* 19 (1992) 165.

[59] Gunton, *Actuality of Atonement,* 88.

[60] Weaver, *Nonviolent Atonement,* 54.

crucifixion. Paul articulates *both* a redeeming death theology and an apocalyptic resurrection theology. Paul creates ulcers for academics by combining cultic and transformative ideas. He cannot be forced into one or the other realm of thinking when he insists on both "Christ crucified" and the "transform[ation] of your minds" (1 Cor 1:23; Rom 12:2).

3.2.4 The Moral Influence Theory

In the generation after Anselm, a professor of theology at the University of Paris, Peter Abelard, rejects all ransom and satisfaction theories: "the purpose and cause of the incarnation was that He might illuminate the world by His wisdom and excite it to the love of Himself."[61]

> How cruel and wicked it seems that anyone should demand the blood of an innocent person as the price for anything, or that it should in any way please him that an innocent man should be slain—still less that God should consider the death of his Son so agreeable that by it he should be reconciled to the whole world![62]

For Abelard, the manner of Christ's death should stimulate in believers repentance and the determination to act rightly. Since the focus is on the subjective effect, this is sometimes called the subjective theory of the atonement, but it is more often identified as the "moral influence" theory. The focus is on the moral effect that Christ's life and death has on the person who honestly reflects upon it: "everyone becomes more righteous—by which we mean a greater lover of God—after the Passion of Christ than before."[63]

Abelard did not share the common assumption of universal guilt, and it may have been this fact that aroused the strongest clerical rage against him, or it may have been that he was so popular among theology students. Bernard of Clairvaux, otherwise known for writing about the love of God, has only hatred for Abelard's approach and devotes himself to getting church councils to condemn Abelard.

Abelard paid attention to certain aspects of salvation that had been neglected for centuries. He saw that real forgiveness had to mean "making the sinner better,"[64] but objective theories of atonement did

---

[61] *Epistle ad Rom.*; Rashdall, *Idea of Atonement*, 358.

[62] *Epistle ad Rom.* 3:19-26; from *A Scholastic Miscellany*, ed. E. R. Fairweather (London: SCM, 1956) 283.

[63] From *A Scholastic Miscellany*, 284.

[64] Rashdall, *Idea of Atonement*, 359.

not suggest that the sinner is changed inwardly at all. Abelard put the emphasis back on the whole of Christ's life, not just its tragic end. The message of his death is no different than the message of his life: he came to *instruct* us in God's love and to inspire us toward receptivity of God's grace.[65] Seeing the noble death of a truly innocent man who bore no ill will "touched the conscience, and regenerated the life of believers"[66] (and of the Roman centurion as well: Mark 15:39).

Heim writes that both the Christus Victor and the moral influence interpretations have biblical roots, but that there is a third approach that finds saving significance in "the incarnation as a whole,"[67] in "God's transit of the fullness of human life—from conception and birth to friendship and struggle. . . . It is God's presence in the human condition that saves. Death is notable only as the most unlikely aspect of that condition for God to share." On the same page, Heim dismisses this as "atonement lite,"[68] but he seems to understand the need for this view. The whole Gospel story matters: Jesus' teachings, his responses to challenges, his sensitivity to particular conversation partners and their needs. The Gospels show many of Jesus' actions and responses having an uplifting, clarifying, and *saving* effect on others, and Jesus thought they did, too. Can we denude the actions and sayings of Jesus of saving significance? Did the Savior have no power to save *during* his Incarnation?

3.2.5 Reformation Theories

Luther's teachings turn out to be considerably more complex than one might realize if one reads only the interpretations of his works by others. He repeats the teachings of Augustine on universal sin and divine rescue but he also (at least in the first half of his writing career) accepts the *theōsis* doctrines of the Greek fathers. His most influential teachings are that salvation is completely undeserved, that it was secured by the death of Christ, and that salvation is by faith alone.

Both Luther and Calvin present a dramatic and frightening scenario of divine violence restrained by divine mercy, but a mercy that had to be mediated through violence. They take it for granted, without ever

---

[65] Passages from Abelard to this effect are in Gorringe, *God's Just Vengeance*, 111.

[66] Rashdall, *Idea of Atonement*, 360.

[67] Called the "physical theory," Kelly with Irenaeus, Origen, Athanasius, and Gregory of Nyssa as exemplars of this view; *Early Christian*, 172–3, 185, 377–8, 381.

[68] S. Mark Heim, "Christ Crucified," in *Christian Century* 118, no. 8 (March 7, 2001) 17.

explaining why, that a sacrificial death was required. Calvin teaches that God is burning with anger at human sin, but that God set up a sacrificial avenue for escape from deserved punishment. He wrote that Christ experienced "all the signs of a wrathful and avenging God."[69] But Luther had already preceded him by having Christ become "the greatest transgressor, murderer, adulterer . . . that ever was or could be" while he was on the cross,[70] lingering on his description of the burning wrath of God against the innocent Son. The Father, in Luther, is always severe. It is the Son who is compassionate. Even when Luther speaks of the Father's love, he also speaks of the Son as "the propitiation for our sins"; through his death, God "is appeased and become our loving Father."[71] There is a negotiation within the divine nature; the Father's wrath has to be placated.

There are some NT passages that speak of believers being predestined to be saved[72] and others that speak of God's "purpose," or of his "sending" the Son.[73] Luther assumes from these that God preplanned the killing of the Son from the beginning of time. Christ was "the Lamb of God ordained from everlasting to take away the sins of the world . . . . wrapped of his own accord in our sins."[74] Still, it is not clear why God had to use a terrible killing as the means for salvation.

Luther stresses God's free will while diminishing human free will. God chooses to save only some people, and there is no explaining God's choice. Yet sinners have no excuse, they deserve damnation. Luther is so pessimistic about human nature that he criticizes priests who ask penitents if they grieve for their sins, since there is no possibility of *real* repentance[75] (that would mean there could be some actual goodness in a human being!).

The prevailing understanding of Luther's theory of justification has always been that he taught that God does not confer *actual* righteousness but only *imputed* righteousness on the believer.[76] But some Finnish

---

[69] *Institutes of the Christian Religion* 2.16.11; from Christina A. Baxter, "The Cursed Beloved: A Reconsideration of Penal Substitution," in *Atonement Today*, ed. John Goldingay (London: SPCK, 1995) 56.

[70] *Commentary on Galatians* 3:13; from Dillenberger, *Martin Luther: Selections*, 135.

[71] *A Commentary on St. Paul's Epistle to the Galatians* 4:19; rev. trans. based on the Middleton English edition (London: James Clarke & Co., 1953) 412.

[72] Rom 8:29; Eph 1:5, 11; Rev 13:8.

[73] Eph 3:11; Gal 4:4; Rom 8:3.

[74] *In Gal.* 3:13; Dillenberger, *Martin Luther*, 137.

[75] Rashdall, *Idea of Atonement*, 402–3.

[76] Sin . . . shall not be imputed unto them, for Christ's sake. . . . Christ hath given himself for it" (*In Gal.* 5:17; Dillenberger, *Martin Luther*, 151–2).

theologians now vigorously dispute such an assessment of Luther,[77] and they quote from various parts of his works to prove this point. They are relying mainly on his early works but also on *The Freedom of a Christian* (1520), written three years into our formal demarcation of the "Reformation." Luther writes,

> Just as the heated iron glows like fire because of the union of fire with it, so the Word imparts its qualities to the soul. . . . Faith unites the soul with Christ as a bride is united with her bridegroom. . . . Christ and the soul become one flesh.[78]

> Faith makes us lords, love makes us servants; aye, through faith we become gods and partakers of the divine nature and name, as Ps 82:6 says: . . . Ye are gods, and all of you are children of the Most High.[79]

None of this, however, reverses the doctrines for which Luther is more famous: all humanity facing damnation, but the Son as innocent substitute, bearing the divine wrath that everyone else deserved. There is no contradiction for Luther between humanity's utter depravity and the promise of deification, which does not come from any human value or worth.

"Faith" is clearly the center of soteriology for Luther, but it is the dogmatic content of faith that he intends. One can neglect love but not belief;[80] he attacks "the wicked gloss of the schoolmen" that faith, to be effective, needs love; Luther thinks such a notion would lead people to think that it is really love, not faith, that justifies.[81]

The pressure of his conflict with the Catholic authorities pushes Luther's expression to extremes, but it also influences the content of his teaching. It is no accident that Simo Peura, who kicked off the current Finnish discussion, did so by evaluating Luther's writings of 1513–19,[82] mostly preceding the open Reformation break. Luther's break with the Roman church leads him further and further away from allowing any goodness to human nature, and leads him to say harsh and bitter things about uniting faith with love. Luther shows us that

[77] Various articles in *Union With Christ: The New Finnish Interpretation of Luther*, ed. C. E. Braaten and R. W. Jensen (Grand Rapids, Mich.: Eerdmans, 1998).

[78] *The Freedom of a Christian*; from Dillenberger, *Martin Luther*, 58, 60.

[79] *On Matthew 8:1-13 7*, from *What Luther Says*, ed. and trans. Ewald M. Plass (St. Louis: Concordia Publishing House, 1959) 1:502 (*Sämmtliche Sch.* 11:481).

[80] *In Gal.* 4:8; 5:9-10; Rashdall, *Idea of Atonement*, 408.

[81] *In Gal.* 2:16; from Dillenberger, *Martin Luther*, 115.

[82] Tuomo Mannermaa, "Why Is Luther So Fascinating? Modern Finnish Luther Research," in *Union With Christ*, 9.

theōsis is not necessarily an alternative to doctrines of divine violence averted by martyrological atonement. Despite the Finnish findings, the doctrines of Luther that have been influential are absolute depravity, universal guilt, and a horrifying transfer of divine wrath to the undeserving Son. When such doctrines sink in, they give rise to severe distress in most believers, ultimately contributing to the rejection of Christianity. Nor is Jean Calvin any different on this score: damnation is everyone's deserved fate. Even babies "are guilty . . . . their whole nature is a seed of sin."[83]

Faced with such monstrous teachings, contemporary theologians are quick to say that atonement is a mystery that cannot be satisfactorily explained but only illustrated—and then promptly try to offer a satisfactory rationalization of this transaction. But the only atonement explanation consistent with the goodness of God is the old rescue theory where God tricks the devil. The problem is that this is not a fully monotheistic theory: God is only slightly more powerful than the devil.

Doctrines of atonement can retain *either* the goodness of God or the full sovereignty of God, but not both. To assert the full sovereignty of God and also the full raft of punishing and substitutionary theology is to rob God of goodness. Luther and Calvin accept this option and take an anti-humanitarian stance to prevent protests from the moral side. Luther recommends that we fully accept the arbitrariness of God even "in damning the undeserving, that is, ungodly persons, who, being born in ungodliness, can by no means avoid being ungodly"; we must be "believing Him just when to us He seems unjust. . . . His justice also should be incomprehensible," and it is "perverse" to try to "evaluate God's judgment!"[84] Luther thought he had to believe in a God who outraged his own deepest moral sensibilities. The ironic result of this is a God who is legalistic in condemning but arbitrarily extralegal in saving, who commands absolute obedience but expects universal rebellion, who justifies a few who do not deserve it and condemns many who are not to blame. Luther asks us to accept that "glory . . . will one day reveal . . . a God Whose justice is most righteous and evident,"[85] but this asks people to repudiate their own best thinking and to maintain a fracture between faith and reason, between belief and

---

[83] *Institutes* 2.1.8; cited by Wilko van Holten, "Can the Traditional View of Hell Be Defended? An Evaluation of Some Arguments for Eternal Punishment," in *ATR* 85 (2003) 473.

[84] *Bondage of the Will* 19; Dillenberger, *Martin Luther*, 200.

[85] *Bondage of the Will* 19; Dillenberger, *Martin Luther*, 202.

values. No wonder some contemporary theologians prefer to return to the more primitive and less than fully monotheistic doctrine. God may be incomplete there, but at least God will not rip one's mind and heart asunder, asking that one's belief go against one's deepest concepts of fairness.

Luther could declare independence from corrupt clerical practices but not from distorted dogma, and certainly not from his own internal conflicts and rage. The position of this important intellectual ends up being anti-intellectual: dogma need not answer to reason; in fact, dogma *must* offend reason or "it clearly would not be Divine."[86] This intellectual hostility to intellect says more about Luther's pained and complicated personal history than it does about God.

As we saw, the sacrificial metaphors that Paul used were simplified and hardened into doctrine, giving us the soteriology that most Christians now take for granted. All of Paul's subtleties, as well as the implication that no one metaphor is sufficient, were forgotten by the later and lesser minds of Christianity. I do not believe that Paul ever intended that one should interpret his metaphors with the crudeness of Gregory the Great or the troubled self-loathing of Luther. Still, Paul's soteriological formulas about the death of Christ[87] provided the seedbed for those frightening and rigid theologies of atonement that came later, even though Paul's own insight greatly transcended that of all his children. That is ironically appropriate, since, in a Semitic worldview, no child is greater than its father. We have certainly suffered from the overly literal way that Paul has been taken, but we cannot absolve Paul of responsibility for the fact that people have brought a transactional interpretation to bear on the idea that God "did not withhold his own Son" (Rom 8:32), and that believers "were bought with a price" (1 Cor 6:20).

3.3 The Psychology of Atonement

3.3.1 Why Atonement Is Compelling

Especially if we are going to question certain staples of Western atonement theology, we need to ask why atonement has been so compelling in religious thought. Nor will it do to give a simplistic answer

---

[86] *Bondage of the Will* 19; Dillenberger, *Martin Luther*, 200.

[87] He certainly reshapes the formulas he "received" (1 Cor 15:3). His restatements reflect *his* soteriology.

such as "Atonement stands for patriarchal violence, and violent men have always ruled the world. End of discussion." Nothing is so simple. Nor does it account for the fact that both violent and nonviolent people have articulated their viewpoints with some version of atonement teaching. The pervasiveness of atonement thinking only makes sense if it incorporates fundamental instincts about reality that are shared by most people. There are certain notions about life, about reciprocity, that are ancestral to the complex of ideas we call atonement. Before there were any complicated theologies, there were bywords and axioms about "the way things are."

Atonement theologies confirm two fundamental and universal instincts about life and about divinity: the belief that nothing is free, that there must be give-and-take in the spiritual economy as there is in the material; and secondly, the intuition that ritual establishes order. To attend to the first point: There seems to be a universal belief or conclusion that the Divinity gives nothing for free; that "man always pays. . . . Death has a *right* to his victims,"[88] so deliverance from death must be matched by a payment or "compensation."[89] There is a "compulsory feeling that somehow compensation should be given."[90] The spirit world is understood to involve a swing between good luck and bad luck or (in a more structured worldview) an economy of debt and debt-elimination through payment. People tend to think about the spiritual realm the same way they think about give-and-take in the material realm.

There is a nearly universal belief that properly constructed ritual has a conserving and restorative function. The purposes of ritual are to affirm the establishment of order, the maintenance of order, and the restoration of order; Yom Kippur, for instance, which annually purifies the temple, is restorative.[91] Cosmically and socially focused "rituals are [a] means of holding back social confusion, indeterminacy, and chaos."[92] Gorman has a knack for summarizing the essence of ritual: "order is achieved through separations and distinctions."[93] "Order is established through the careful observation of categorical divisions."[94]

---

[88] H. S. Versnel, "Self-Sacrifice, Compensation, and the Anonymous Gods," in *Le Sacrifice dans l'Antiquité* (Geneva: Vandoeuvres, 1980) 179, 178.

[89] Versnel, "Self-Sacrifice," 169.

[90] Ibid., 185.

[91] Gorman, *Ideology of Ritual*, 59, 61.

[92] Ibid., 29.

[93] Ibid., 80.

[94] Ibid., 45.

Atonement ideas that emerge from sacrificial cult, then, reflect ancient intuitions about getting something from the god (purification, favor) and giving something to the god (animal and vegetable foodstuffs).

Sacrifice also responds to a perceived need for ritual purification (restoration of order). Ritual restores one's adequacy before God by reinstating proper hierarchy and order, and it even retains this function when it is spiritualized—when it is purely metaphorical. Sacrificial soteriology offers ritual rectification of the condition of spiritual corruption, thus offering relief to the one who is conscious of being stained with sin or standing in irredeemable spiritual debt (both of which are forms of disorder).

Underneath the shining sun of Christian triumphal faith, then, is the gloom of this ancient consciousness of *being stained*, which plays itself out in the extreme actions of ascetic saints and troubled believers throughout the centuries. Paul is not alien to his contemporaries (or his successors) in this matter, but Jesus was profoundly ill at ease with purity boundaries, as is shown by his behavior in the Temple, his several times quoting the most radical prophets, and his deliberate consorting with "unclean" Gentiles, women, and tax collectors. Jesus was repeatedly criticized by religious professionals and politicians for disregarding purity boundaries.[95]

Is my interpretation overly modernizing and negative about atonement (as I have been told)? Would it not make sense to look at the ways that atonement has proven useful to people, how it has been linked to their moral development (as I myself have asked)? As people grow through adolescence into adulthood, they learn that they cannot always get what they want, and that getting is always related to giving. In relations with friends and with adults, young people learn that sharing is usually a matter of giving and receiving and limiting one's demands. Adults learn that long-term relationships mean channeling one's sexual appetite to one partner. Husbands and wives both make concessions to allow the marriage to work. The idea of "making sacrifices," then, is a necessary part of moral development. There is certainly some truth in this, but it is fairly pedestrian truth. God is not just another superior with whom we must *deal*. Atonement doctrines turn God into a heavenly judge, an offended lord, or a temperamental spirit. The notion of "paying" God to undo a penalty is materialistic.

---

[95] See section 4.6.2.

The notion that all sin carries a penalty certainly has moral worth, but it represents the adolescent stage of moral development. An adult must question those mundane learned lessons of life and see which ones are worthy of retention and which need modification. Some of them (especially the ones about the rights of superiors) are really the product of particular social structures and will change when the social structures change. The harshness of God is largely a byproduct of the harshness of parents and other authorities. As parents become less frightening figures, God becomes less frightening.

"Our sense that the ritual deals with our guilt and inadequacy is instinctive."[96] But can we afford to be always led about by ancient instincts?

3.3.2 The Guilt-Gratitude Cycle

Redemption-sacrificial doctrine perpetuates intense anxiety about a temperamental and judgmental God, firing a cycle of outbursts of rage or guilt, blame or self-blame. Superstition is a wolf that dons the sheep's clothing of "selfless sacrifice" and "innocent blood" and so enters into Christian theology and wreaks havoc in one generation after another. People learn to develop strategies of bargaining, appeasement, diversion, and payment through self-punishment and pain—each of which is manipulative. These strategies were played out in great detail in the Middle Ages in penances, self-flagellations, promises of building chapels, and other attempts at negotiation with God, none of which reflects the simple Gospel teaching that disciples should *trust* God who delights in giving every good thing to God's children (Matt 6:30-33; 7:7-11). This God need not be manipulated.

The intense Reformation focus on guilt followed by undeserved rescue from destruction leaves a powerful and painful psychological legacy. Appealing to the emotions of guilt and gratitude, this teaching encourages an experience of repentance. Contemplation of the great Sacrifice arouses feelings of dread and guilt. Confession and liturgy bring relief, for a time, through a (metaphoric) ritual of expiation—a ritual that eventually came to consist entirely of *affirming* certain statements of doctrine. The affective (feeling) corollary of the beliefs is a pattern of shame, release, and submissive gratitude. Release from

---

[96] Frances Young, *Sacrifice and the Death of Christ* (Cambridge: Cambridge University Press, 1975) 109.

doom at the hands of God produces feelings of gratitude, but even more of *indebtedness*. The atonement doctrine, even while it replaces the actual sacrificial ritual, perpetuates the sacrificial beliefs and emotions.

Rationalization of atonement doctrine is both spurred by anxiety and drawn on by love motivated by selfishness *and* by selflessness. This is the painful irony about atonement: it draws together the most noble and the most crudely selfish of motives. Simplistic analysis simply will not do justice to this topic; atonement commingles both the noble and the cruel.

The sacrificial interpretation of the death of Jesus takes ancient ideas of ritual pollution, blood-magic, sin-debt, and ransoming, and spiritualizes them with ideas of heroism and (sometimes) of moral repair. The result is a complicated mix of traditions and instincts with an attitude toward cult that is simultaneously supersessionist and yet still cultic. The cult is dead, long live the cult!—abstractly, and internalized in an intensely emotional way.

There are many strategies for rescuing, toning down, or restating atonement in ways that are palatable to present-day audiences. The next chapter examines some of these approaches.

4

Rationalizing the Atonement Doctrine

For the last 250 years, popular notions of atonement have caused embarrassment among Christians who recoil from the idea that the Son's death was either a kind of payment or a divinely demanded penalty. Yet this image refuses to depart from Christian discourse. This is because manipulative and magical ideas are inherent in the genetic ancestry of the cultic and redemption metaphors that have become not just the vehicles but the content-providers of Christian teaching.

Most theologians claim to accept the prophetic principle that God cannot be persuaded through sacrificial offerings. Yet precisely this is implied in all doctrines of intercessory atonement. Many of the defenders of these doctrines seem not to recognize the violence implicit in them. Others are aware of it, but have their reasons for wanting to defend what they think is central Christian doctrine against criticism. A considerable number of writers try to tame, spiritualize, improve, and update atonement. Some take an old concept (such as "redemption") and empty it of its traditional content, pouring in more modern and humane-sounding content.[1]

In this chapter, I will examine a number of different responses to, and spiritualizations of, atonement teachings, starting out with some writers who appear to recommend one of the traditional formulations but whose arguments reveal that they, too, have problems with the doctrine.

---

[1] "Redemption involves the higher *integration* . . . . between bodily existence and spiritual orientation" (Crysdale, *Embracing Travail*, 146).

4.1 Restating Atonement

Robert Sherman has attempted a trinitarian approach to the atonement. He correlates the threefold office of Christ (king, priest, prophet) with the three Persons of the Trinity and also with the three standard theories of the atonement, arguing that the Christus Victor theory goes with the royal Father, vicarious sacrifice goes with the priestly Son, and the moral example theory goes with the (prophetic) Holy Spirit.[2] This theory is more elegant than it is clarifying. For Sherman, the test of any atonement theory is whether it somehow can be correlated with the Trinity. The satisfaction theory, which Calvin himself correlated with the threefold office of Christ, is therefore rescued from criticism.[3]

Simply distinguishing the Persons of the Trinity does not solve the problems with atonement; in fact, it may heighten them by setting one Person of the Trinity against another. Richard of St. Victor wrote, "The Father punishes, the Son expiates, the Spirit forgives (*ignosceret*) . . . the Father demands satisfaction, the Son pays it, and the Spirit interposes between."[4] Here, Trinitarianism asserts conflict within God. The idea of the kindness of the Son paying off the pride of the Father can hardly be good for the development of Christian ethics.

Sherman keeps the judgmental role of the Father toned down, but that is precisely what was front and center for many Christian theologians from Augustine to Luther: the Father was a frightening figure. Jesus not only saves us from condemnation but from *God's anger* (something that needs no courtroom to manifest itself). Sherman does not ask any really challenging questions about the satisfaction theory. We are still left wondering why the innocent Son had to be murdered before any pardon could be issued. What kind of judge requires punishment but is content to allow the punishment of the innocent? Sherman's avoidance of the hard questions seems to cover up his secret problems with the doctrine.

More common than such book-length efforts are articles that piously give a nod to atonement, restating or spiritualizing it, but leaving the logic tangled and confused. David Wheeler tries to spiritualize the scapegoat ritual by moralizing thus:

[2] Robert Sherman, *King, Priest, and Prophet: A Trinitarian Theology of Atonement* (New York: T & T Clark, 2004) 15–6, 23.

[3] Sherman, *King, Priest,* 66–75.

[4] Richard of St. Victor, *De Verbo Incarnato* 11 (PL 196:1005), in Gorringe, *God's Just,* 116. Here, "satisfaction theory seems to pit the mercy and justice of God against each other" (Gorringe, 145), perceived in the Middle Ages as an advantage, but now (correctly) recognized to be a liability.

> Blood is life . . . . Life costs . . . . Aaron confesses over the goat . . .
> and sends it away. . . . . Is there not a "dying" of offended pride and a
> dismissing of resentment that occurs when reconciliation is pursued?
> The offended party cedes their right to be aggrieved, perhaps at great
> cost.[5]

Exactly what equation is he making here? That forgiveness means becoming a victim? Is he equating forgiveness with passivity and indifference to one's welfare? Apparently it is not necessary to be clear when using substitutionary metaphors; the mere allusion to a cultic death is considered sufficient. Can we not have a more just and sane approach? Cannot a teaching of reconciliation be made without recommending becoming a scapegoat?

Even more unaccountable are the views of P. J. Fitzpatrick who says he is well aware "of the dangers that lie in the crudity" of the substitutionary doctrine, yet he hopes that, "by means of selective amnesia and inspired inattention, it is possible for believers to profit by credal [sic] and devotional forms that, taken at their face-value, are indefensible."[6] How can this convoluted strategy be reconciled with the principle that "the truth will make you free" or with the straightforward instruction that if something is harmful it should be cut off? If Euripides could protest against the notions of a goddess demanding human sacrifice and of the gods sitting down, unawares, at a cannibalistic feast,[7] surely we can protest against turning Jesus' Father (and "*your* Father"[8]) into a sacrifice-demanding deity. Are Christians less theologically sensitive than a pagan playwright? How can an honest Christian really think that the best strategy regarding the biggest problems in the Christian tradition is deliberate deception?

It is time to move on to more serious efforts.

4.2 Redefining Sacrifice

One of the key strategies for dealing with atonement is to redefine the practice that underlies the metaphor: sacrifice. If the underlying

---

[5] David L. Wheeler, "The Cross and the Blood: Dead or Living Images?" in *Dialog* 35 (1996) 11–2.

[6] P. J. Fitzpatrick, "On Eucharistic Sacrifice in the Middle Ages," in *Sacrifice and Redemption: Durham Essays in Theology*, ed. S. Sykes (Cambridge: Cambridge University Press, 1991) 153.

[7] *Iph. taur.*, lines 386–98; from *Ten Plays by Euripides*, Hadas and McLean, 251.

[8] Matt 5:16, 45, 48; 6:8, 14; Luke 6:36; John 20:17.

metaphor means something different than has been thought, then Christian soteriology can be understood differently than it has been in the past.

4.2.1 Sacrifice as Soul-Repair

A bold spiritualization of sacrifice is gaining prominence in German scholarship. Avoiding the judicial metaphor and bringing out some deep implications of the Incarnation is Otfried Hofius who states that Christ died while *living in the human place*, not as a substitute *in place of* humans. Christ lives a human life, shares a human fate. This is "inclusive place-taking"[9]—humans are included, not excluded, in Christ's representative life. In Christ, God lived in a human place. Hofius finds this "divine" place-taking in the Levitical sacrificial cult, but not in the actions of the Suffering Servant of Isaiah 53, which depict only "exclusive place-taking."[10]

Hofius is picking up on the argument of his mentor, Hartmut Gese, who writes that sacrifice "was to deal with the depraved *being* of humans. . . . [T]he damaged being is reconstructed and healed."[11] Gese sees an act of self-surrender in the ritual: "atonement [i]s a total substitutionary commitment of a life."[12] One might almost forget that it is the *animal* who has to do the dying! "Atonement is the sacrifice of life for the sake of making life whole."[13] For me, this is the textbook example of Level Two Spiritualization: he Christianizes and philosophizes the ancient ritual. "Through the shedding of the animal's blood the life of the person who brings the sacrifice is symbolically offered up. . . . This sacrifice of life . . . is . . . an incorporation into the holy."[14] Gese says the sacrifice-critical Psalms 40 and 51 are "the complete internalization of the thank offering . . . . not . . . critique of sacrifice, but rather the total involvement of the person in the essence of sacrifice."[15]

[9] Otfried Hofius, "The Fourth Servant Song in the New Testament Letters," in *The Suffering Servant: Isaiah 53 in Jewish and Christian Sources*, ed. Bernd Janowski and Peter Stuhlmacher, trans. Daniel P. Bailey (Grand Rapids, Mich.: Eerdmans, 2004) 173–5; Daniel P. Bailey, "Concepts of *Stellvertretung* in the Interpretation of Isaiah 53," in *Jesus and the Suffering Servant: Isaiah 53 and Christian Origins*, ed. William H. Bellinger Jr. and William R. Farmer (Harrisburg, Penn.: Trinity, 1998) 241.

[10] Hofius, "Fourth Servant," 170; Bailey, "Concepts of *Stellvertretung*," 241–2.

[11] Hartmut Gese, *Essays on Biblical Theology* (Minneapolis: Augsburg, 1981) 110.

[12] Ibid., 106.

[13] Ibid., 115.

[14] Ibid., 107.

[15] Ibid., 132.

Gese seems to think that all the glory of the new covenant was already contained in the cultic law of the old covenant, but Paul said that the glory of the old covenant was fading away, being surpassed by the glory of the new (2 Cor 3:10-11). Gese places all his eggs in the cultic basket, and by so doing, distances himself from the orthodox Christian tradition, although he thinks he is affirming it. But none of the apostles or church fathers saw atonement in *strictly* cultic categories; they saw the OT as fundamentally prophetic: cult mattered because of its typological implication. The OT was not seen as a finished story, but a prophecy of the Messianic story. This is one of the meanings of Paul's "Christ is the end of the law" (Rom 10:4)—*end (telos)* is goal or fulfillment. By taking the effectiveness of the Jewish cult literally, Gese has returned to a pre-Christian understanding of atonement. In fact, he tries to take theology back to the time before Hellenistic spiritualizing had begun—and yet he ignores the most interesting ethical voices from that time: the prophets.

Following some of these cues, but paying closer attention to the method of the authors of the NT epistles, Hofius says, "there is not a single passage where the fourth Servant Song has been taken up in its original sense," but it has been given an atoning and christological interpretation.[16] Hofius sees the Gospel utilizing nothing of the ethics of Second Isaiah. Only atonement, and not the fellow-suffering of the Servant, is relevant: "being freed up from sin and guilt through *human* substitution is theologically simply unthinkable!"[17] It is the sin-offering and not Isaiah 53 or any other prophetic message that symbolizes inclusive place-taking.[18] The gesture of identification over the sacrificial animal is the key moment of contact with the divine.[19]

I must ask: Does the Incarnation find its only precursor in *a cultic gesture*? Does the Isaianic idea of compassionate burden-bearing count for nothing? Hofius ignores instances of divine sharing in human suffering described in Second Isaiah: "I have taken you by the hand. . . . When you pass through the waters, I will be with you . . . . it is the Lord God who helps me . . . . For your Maker is your husband" (42:6; 43:2; 50:9; 54:5). Is this not inclusive place-taking?

---

[16] Hofius, "Fourth Servant," 187–8.

[17] Ibid., 172.

[18] Otfried Hofius, *Paulusstudien*. WUNT 51 (Tübingen: J.C.B. Mohr [Paul Siebeck], 1989) 40–4; Bailey, "Concepts of *Stellvertretung*," 242–4. The cultic basis of "inclusive place-taking" is largely concealed in Hofius's "Fourth Servant," but is detectable on 174 and in notes 44 and 46, where he relies on Gese's spiritualization of the OT cult.

[19] Hofius, *Paulusstudien*, 42–3, repeatedly referring to Gese.

Starting out with a noble insight (God's "inclusive place-taking"), Gese and Hofius end up affirming a magical concept of salvation. This revalorization of sacrificial cult for its own sake is a step into the past when the favor of the gods required meticulous adherence to cultic procedure. This approach overvalues the Levitical cult, suffocates the voices of the prophets, suppresses the Isaianic demand for fellow-feeling and heroic action, and fails to say anything about Christ's own teaching.

4.2.2 Sacrifice as Sacred Violence

4.2.2.1 The Theory of Girard

While Hofius sets out to exonerate sacrifice from negative connotations, Girard condemns sacrifice but exonerates the NT from having any sacrificial imagery. It is a nearly opposite strategy from Hofius's, then, for it rejects the sacrificial system as being violent and murderous. Girard's theory is that sacrifice encodes violence. Sacrifice evolved out of, and conceals, an underlying pattern of violent persecution of (human) scapegoats.

Girard's understanding of religion and violence is the product of decades of reflection on "mimetic desire" (which I would call imitative envy) where people learn to desire what their peers (and rivals) desire. He began by noticing the behavior of rival "doubles" in literature, where one character learns to desire what his rival desires.[20] Girard moved on to study mimetic desire and violence in mythology and ritual. He came to the conclusion that humanity is dominated by mimetic desire, and that most social violence arises out of intense desire and competition. Humanity is afflicted with a pattern of mimetic desire that builds up and erupts into violence, threatening social safety and stability.

> The idolization of the neighbor . . . . is necessarily associated with the idolization of ourselves. The more desperately we seek to worship ourselves and to be good "individualists," the more compelled we are to worship our rivals in a cult that turns to hatred. . . . The principal source of violence between human beings is mimetic rivalry, the rivalry resulting from imitation of a model who becomes a rival or of a rival who becomes a model.[21]

---

[20] One copies "a mass of behaviors, attitudes, things learned, prejudices, preferences" (René Girard, *I See Satan Fall Like Lightning*, trans. James G. Williams [Maryknoll, N.Y.: Orbis, 2001] 15).

[21] Girard, *I See Satan*, 11.

Society always takes action to preserve itself. Tribes and societies the world around, says Girard, learned to channel violent energy onto a victim (a "scapegoat"), thus releasing the rage that threatened society. The memory of these outbursts of mob action is then suppressed by the generation of a mythology that covers it with "sacredness." It was just this kind of "sacred violence" that was directed against Jesus. "A war of all against one . . . is not limited solely to the case of Jesus. . . . The Passion is typical rather than unique."[22]

Human religions are universally guilty of collusion in this scapegoating process. Religious mythology is an organized lie, covering up the violence of the community, "disguising the fact that it is a ritual murder."[23] The sacrificial cult arose as a substitute for scapegoating; so sacrifice symbolizes and disguises the age-old scapegoating mechanism. The sacrificial victim is a substitute for the scapegoat. This assertion has no evidence to support it, of which I am aware, but it is a necessary piece in the Girardian argument.

The OT, Girard says, began the work of exposing and opposing this violent pattern. The Ten Commandments end by prohibiting envy, "the key to the violence prohibited in the four commandments that precede it. If we ceased to desire the goods of our neighbor we would never commit murder or adultery or theft or false witness."[24] Isaiah 53 had begun to expose the scapegoat mechanism in its discussion of the Suffering Servant, but it did not go far enough, since the author says that it is God who made the Servant suffer.[25]

It is the Gospel story that finally exposes all the violence and mythology. It does not excuse or mystify the violence.

> There is nothing in the Gospels to suggest that God causes the mob to come together against Jesus. Violent contagion is enough. Those responsible for the Passion are the human participants themselves.[26]

Jesus himself exposes and repudiates the victimization mechanism. Girard appeals to John 8, where those who are plotting Jesus' murder are said to be following their "father's desires" (8:44a). "They take the devil as the *model* for their desires."[27] They are following a model of envy and

---

[22] Ibid., 22, 28.
[23] Girard's position restated by Weaver, *Nonviolent Atonement*, 47–8.
[24] Girard, *I See Satan*, 11–2.
[25] René Girard, *Things Hidden Since the Foundation of the World* (London: Athlone, 1987) 157; Gorringe, *God's Just Vengeance*, 49.
[26] Girard, *I See Satan*, 21.
[27] Ibid., 40.

violence who lies about his violence afterward. "He was a murderer from the beginning . . . because there is no truth in him" (John 8:44b). Desire, murder, and lying, in that order, are clearly "corresponding to the stages of the mimetic cycle."[28] Christians have often misunderstood or even rejected the message of John 8 because they have not understood the pattern of mimetic rivalry and violence to which they, too, are subject. "The Gospel of John scandalizes those who do not detect in it the choice it implies."[29] Jesus is exposing the motivation of the violence-bound *crowd*.

The Crucifixion, then, is meant to open our eyes to our human patterns of violence and subsequent mythologizing about violence. "The martyrdom of the innocent carpenter . . . reveals the oppressiveness . . . of seeking self-justification through persecution of others."[30] And because sacrificial ritual has been a way of disguising this whole pattern of persecution, the sacrificial interpretation of Christ's death is a great misinterpretation[31] because it sees God as colluding in the continued selection of victims. That is what *people* do. God is not the source of human violence or rationalizations of violence.

These insights are powerful and have exegetical, as well as ethical, validity. My problem with the theory is that it is simplistic, not that there is no pattern of scapegoating and lying. But the theory encourages simplistic and unduly cynical conclusions:

> All religion is essentially a cloak for human violence.[32]
> Violence is the controlling agent in every . . . cultural structure.[33]

This reductionistic theory about the origins of culture and religion can hardly stand up under scrutiny and that is fortunate, since one could only hate the human race if it were true. (But how would such disgust be possible if all society is trained in the scapegoat mentality?)

Girard has a single-issue anthropology of religion. It is incredibly narrow to say that the only factor that mattered in the formation of human religion was the focused release of community rage and envy onto a victim. Evidence from around the world shows religious interest in many

---

[28] Ibid., 41.

[29] Ibid., 42.

[30] Ted Peters, "Sin, Scapegoating, and Justifying Faith," in *Dialog* 39 (2000) 90.

[31] Girard, *Things Hidden*, 183; Gorringe, *God's Just Vengeance*, 68.

[32] Robert G. Hamerton-Kelly, "Sacred Violence and Sinful Desire: Paul's Interpretation of Adam's Sin," in *The Conversation Continues: Studies in Paul and John in Honor of J. Louis Martyn*, ed. Robert T. Fortna and Beverly R. Gaventa (Nashville: Abingdon, 1990) 38.

[33] Girard, *Things Hidden*, 219.

subjects both practical and speculative, from concern about the food supply to hope for an afterlife, and everything in between: anxiety about disease; interest in ethics and law; concepts of give-and-take, bargaining, and exchange; reflection on order, hierarchy, separation, honor, shame, power, loyalty, and obligation; and intuitions about spirits and angels. An adequate theory about the causes of religion and culture can hardly ignore these factors or proceed on a theory of a *single* kind response to internal social violence. What about other responses to potential internal violence such as compromise, arbitration, reparation, gift exchange, athletic combat, heroic questing, and war against outsiders?

Girard's single-issue concern with scapegoating is best explained by noticing that it emerged in Europe in the immediate aftermath of the Holocaust; it is a noble and expected response of an ethically sensitive person to the monstrous program of scapegoating undertaken by the Nazis, but it is inadequate as a theory of the origin of religion. Further, if correct, it means that all people are nothing but violent hypocrites, and how could the Gospel change or save such creatures? If it is true, "that in all human institutions it is necessary to reproduce a reconciliatory murder by means of new victims,"[34] what possible hope could there be for ethical change?

Girard's theory is so radical, that it is difficult to remain fully Girardian, and Girard himself has backed off from the sharpness of this kind of remark.[35] If one is to be a genuine Girardian, one must notice that, "Girard . . . fails to see through the radical consequences of his own thought."[36] Girard fails to apply the critique (sufficiently) to Christianity itself.[37]

One *can* criticize sacred violence and violent atonement doctrine without being "Girardian" if one recognizes that the theory is simplistic in its assertions about a universal scapegoat mechanism. The problems of human violence and the contents of human religions are considerably more complicated than Girard allows.

---

[34] Ibid., 53.

[35] "I scapegoated the word 'sacrifice'" (Girard, "Violence, Difference, Sacrifice: A Conversation with René Girard," Rebecca Adams interview. *Religion and Literature* 25.2 [1993] 19); cf. Bartlett, *Cross Purposes*, 12.

[36] Bartlett, *Cross Purposes*, 14.

[37] "Christianity is largely spared in Girard" (Bartlett, *Cross Purposes*, 40); Bartlett wants to understand "Christian violence, particularly in reference to atonement doctrine and its validation of sacred violence" (10). But Girard does critique "the sacrificial theology of Christianity" (*Things Hidden*, 227; cf. 180–2, 224–30).

Further, there is a potentially fatal contradiction in what Girard says about the Cross. He has God making use of the act of violence against Jesus, turning it around and exposing the "scapegoat mechanism" in human society.[38] But this may re-ensconce the scapegoat mechanism on the divine level if it implies that God did order *one* scapegoat event, as some of Girard's disciples have concluded (see below). But one is one too many. For Girard's analysis to work, it needs to reject *every* instance of scapegoating and not to reestablish scapegoating by attaching it to just one death instead of to thousands.

Nevertheless, Girard's theory is necessary and timely, exposing a behavior that social groups do indeed disguise from themselves and that has often been practiced by religious hierarchies. The Jewish Sanhedrin determined that it was for the good of society "to have one man die for the people" (John 11:50). Christian synods have repeatedly turned their wrath upon honest religious dissenters. Girardian exegetes are among the most astute at analyzing both the violent stories in the OT[39] and the rejection of divine violence by other biblical authors.[40]

It is human nature to imitate our associates and peers, but this can be put to proper use: "What Jesus invites us to imitate is his own *desire*, the spirit that directs him toward the goal on which his intention is fixed: to resemble God the Father as much as possible."[41] There is a way out of our unhealthy mimesis.

Ted Peters provides an updated account of the Girardian thesis about violence. He finds it taking the form of a morally smug in-group looking down upon those outside its group. "Only when we wake up to realize how we participate in the structure of moral self-justification and its concomitant scapegoating will we be able to recognize that our virtues are as sinful as our vices."[42] "Morality becomes the chief weapon used to bludgeon the scapegoat."[43] "Cursing is meant to degrade people, to classify them as pollution."[44]

---

[38] "In triggering the victim mechanism against Jesus, Satan . . . . did exactly what God had foreseen. . . . The divine wisdom knew . . . . he would participate in God's plan unawares" (*I See Satan*, 151–2).

[39] James G. Williams, *The Bible, Violence, and the Sacred: Liberation from the Myth of Sanctioned Violence* (San Francisco: Harper, 1991) 52–3, 120–6.

[40] Regarding the "prophetic resistance to violence," see Williams, *The Bible*, 118, 150–61.

[41] Girard, *I See Satan*, 13.

[42] Ted Peters, *Sin: Radical Evil in Soul and Society* (Grand Rapids, Mich.: Eerdmans, 1994) 178.

[43] Peters, "Sin, Scapegoating," 88.

[44] Peters, *Sin: Radical*, 168.

4.2.2.2 Exonerating Paul

Since Girardian theory holds that the NT never perpetuates sacrificial or scapegoat mythology, Robert Hamerton-Kelly tries to protect Paul from sacrificial thinking: "Paul's interpretation is moral, not sacrificial."[45] Actually, Paul's interpretation is *both* moral and sacrificial, not always with full consistency. Paul does expose the violence at the heart of society but he also utilizes and perpetuates the scapegoat mechanism (in metaphor) by asserting that God "made" Jesus "to be sin." And Hamerton-Kelly partly acknowledges this. He says, regarding the

> myth of scapegoating, if Paul had carried through to the end the project of demythification started by the Cross, he would have decoded [it] . . . . Atonement . . . shift[s] responsibility for our sins onto the divine . . . . to the effect that God persecuted the Son because of humanity's sin. This God is the primitive Sacred, who takes part with the group in the killing of the victim.[46]

Hamerton-Kelly rejects the distortion of blaming God for the lynching of Jesus and rejects the notion that God required that death. But he minimizes the extent to which Paul implied exactly those things:

> For Paul the primary saving effect of the Cross is as a disclosure of religious violence, not as a sacrificial transaction that appeases the divine wrath. . . . Paul inverts the traditional understanding of sacrifice so that God is the offerer, not the receiver, and the scapegoat goes into the sacred precinct rather than out of it. Christ is a divine offering to humankind, not a human offering to God. . . . It is not God who needs to be propitiated, but humanity.[47]

Even if it were possible to conceive of God appeasing humanity, sacrificial blood-magic is still present! This is not a release from the sacrificial mentality. God is still trapped in the sacrificial system if God has to go through this ritual. In the same book, Hamerton-Kelly does admit that Paul's "metaphors are transformations of sacrificial violence, more or less concealing the founding mechanism . . . . advanc[ing] . . . in the direction of diagnosis."[48] This is a fair assessment, and a needed correc-

---

[45] Robert G. Hamerton-Kelly, *Sacred Violence: Paul's Hermeneutic of the Cross* (Minneapolis: Augsburg Fortress, 1992) 125. He is following Girard's lead (*Things Hidden*, 192–3).

[46] Hamerton-Kelly, *Sacred Violence*, 138–9; cf. 37.

[47] Ibid., 79–80.

[48] Ibid., 115.

tive to Girard. But the earlier remark, about God propitiating humanity, is a slide back into substitutionary mythology. Ted Peters echoes this peculiar reasoning about God both opposing and utilizing sacrifice:

> God does not demand sacrifice. We do . . . . It is we, the human race, who are appeased by the shedding of blood; and it is God who offers it. This shocking reversal reveals that the mechanism of sacrifice had been illegitimate right from the beginning.[49]

Is it not bitterly ironic and contradictory to have God opposing sacrifice all along but utilizing the death of Jesus *as a sacrifice*? It means God used violence this one time. It is one thing to say that God wanted to expose the evil pattern after it happened, but the above expressions imply two additional things: (a) that God sent Jesus to die, and (b) that God then responded to the event as to a sacrificial gift-payment. The first one threatens the values for which Girard is arguing but the second one destroys them utterly. We cannot say that sacrificial violence is illegitimate and also have God taking part in a sacrificial murder. Disclosing to people their patterns of lies and violence was indeed part of Jesus' teaching, but if we make God a co-conspirator in the murder of the Son, we slander God and perpetuate the ancient pattern of blaming God for everything that happens.

Williams speaks of "the revelation of a God who sides with the victims and who summons people to become disengaged from sacrifice."[50] But we have to say that Paul's disengagement is only partial, since he reengages the *ideas* of sacrifice and scapegoat to express soteriology. We have already seen Hamerton-Kelly admit to this while trying to downplay it. To be consistent, Paul should be categorized with the author of Isaiah 53, who is recognized by Girardians as partially exposing, and partially perpetuating, the victimization myth: "It was the will of the Lord to crush him with pain" (Isa 53:10; cf. vv. 4, 6).

In order to escape the unpleasant implications of the wrath of God in Paul's teaching,[51] several scholars perform a gymnastic move with it, making the wrath of God refer to mimetic rivalry: "Wrath is not the active divine vengeance but the effects of sacred violence in the human world."[52] It is "an impersonal force," and thus not sacrificial in con-

---

[49] Peters, "Atonement and the Final," 181.

[50] James G. Williams, "Steadfast Love and Not Sacrifice," in *Curing Violence*, ed. Mark I. Wallace and Theophilus H. Smith. Forum Facsimiles 3 (Sonoma, Calif.: Polebridge Press, 1994) 98.

[51] 1 Thess 1:10; 2:16; Rom 1:18; 5:9; Col 3:6.

[52] Hamerton-Kelly, *Sacred Violence*, 81.

cept.[53] This is a spiritualizing move; wrath has always been recognized as something personal. God's wrath is a significant factor at least in 1 Thessalonians and Romans. Paul does not have the vindictiveness and moral smugness of many later Christians, but retaliation from God is indeed envisioned.

The fact is, both the problematic aspects of atonement *and* the effective answer to those problems are found in the Bible. The Bible is part of the problem . . . and *most* of the solution. We have reached a stage in theological development when we need to acknowledge that the Bible is full of diverse viewpoints and admit that it is not likely to be a transcript straight from the mind of God, though it may indeed be the heavily filtered *human* reflection of the mind of God, a record of the gradual and partial human reception of God's initiatives.

Some biblical passages reflect ancient ideas that cannot any longer be taken literally, while others challenge superstition, cultic literalism, and national pride, emphasizing instead the ethical imperative and the approachability of God. Some authors preserve and articulate certain cultic ideas while also emphatically arguing for ethics and for the nearness of God (I am thinking of Deuteronomy, Ezekiel, Malachi, and Paul).

4.3 Critiques of Atonement

Here I treat some scholars who attempt to clear away what they consider systematic distortion within Christian theories of atonement. We will again encounter the ideas of Girard in this section.

4.3.1 Winter's Critique of Inadequate Atonement Theories

Michael Winter's book is notable for its frank criticism of the inadequate explanations of atonement offered by theologians and scholars. Winter points out how often these explanations are "merely a restatement."[54] For instance, Gustaf Aulén says that God restores human life by undergoing the forces of alienation, but this is not explained (Ibid.). Similarly, Colin Gunton speaks of reconciliation but does not say how it "was actually brought about." Hengel says God identifies himself with the suffering Jesus, "and in so doing overcomes guilt," but "one would dearly like to know what lies behind the words 'in so doing

---

[53] Bartlett, *Cross Purposes*, 204.
[54] Michael Winter, *The Atonement*. Problems in Theology (Collegeville: Liturgical Press, 1995) 35.

overcomes guilt.'"[55] The mechanism of "reconciling" or "overcoming" is left unclear. Again, T. F. Torrance says that Jesus' death was not a moral or legal transaction but he does not spell out what it *was*.[56] Of course, it may be that full explanations are not forthcoming because they would entail ideas of a sacrifice-demanding or payment-demanding God, something difficult for theologians nowadays to argue (and which Paul himself never argues at length), but Winter does not raise this possibility.

Winter offers his own explanation, which is that Jesus is an inter-cessor (Rom 8:34; Heb 7:25) pleading for humanity's forgiveness.[57] This special role seems to be derivative from Jesus' divinity, though the exact kind of intercession involved is not spelled out—as a sort of in-dependent counsel, an officer of the court? as a witness (which is what *martyr* means)? as God's chief advisor? The looming judgment of God is still present if there is a need for an intercessor; and there is a certain savagery involved if this intercessor had to become a substitute victim. But Winter does not tell us exactly what function Jesus plays in the divine law court.

The problem is not what all this says about Jesus but what it says about God: if God wants to save, why is intercession necessary?[58] Why should Jesus' pleading for humanity only be effective after he had been murdered? Why could not this intercession be effective without Jesus being tortured and killed? It does us no good to perceive Jesus as heroic if we are forced to view God as sadistic. This nightmarish sce-nario haunts Christian theology, even when Herculean efforts are made to deny it, and to salvage the loving kindness of God in the face of God's (alleged) need for a victim.

What Winter cannot bring himself to say is that magical thinking obliterates the notion of God as free-willed, and that all transactional thinking weakens the notion of God as just. If the innocent Son *had* to be murdered before the doors of salvation could be opened, this calls God's free will, justice, *and* sanity into question:

Free will—Was God unable to offer forgiveness until the required ritual pattern had been fulfilled?

---

[55] Winter, *The Atonement*, 35.

[56] Ibid., 36–7.

[57] Ibid., 108–13, 133.

[58] At least three readers of Winter have asked this question: Craig L. Nessan ("Vio-lence and Atonement," in *Dialog* 35 [1996] 30 n. 18); Sherman, *King, Priest*, 34; John McIntyre (review of Michael Winter, *The Atonement*, in *SJT* 49 [1996] 124).

Justice—What kind of judge makes pardons conditional upon some new crime being committed? Is God a corrupt judge, whose grant of pardon must be purchased?

Sanity—Does God require a ritual killing? Is God a loving Father, as Jesus taught, but only part of the time, responding to ritual atrocities the rest of the time? Did this Being first endow us with moral capacities and then endorse an atrocity that makes us recoil in horror?

What does magic cleansing or blood-payment have to do with the loving and straight-dealing father of whom Jesus spoke? When he spoke of God knowing what people need and giving it to them,[59] ritual—let alone ritual *violence*—never entered into the discussion.

What kind of reasoning lurks beneath the surface of atonement doctrine, and what kind of harsh and troubled individuals have been its foremost advocates? Atonement is a strange marriage of primitive concepts of a violent god and the revealed teaching of a loving God. Can this marriage of an ancient idea (atonement) and a newer one (God's love) endure? Was it a mismatch from the start, a pouring of new wine into old wineskins?

4.3.2 Weaver: Improving the Atonement

Popular notions of atonement among Christians combine Augustine's, Anselm's, and Luther's theories of the conciliation of divine wrath, the Crucifixion functioning as a kind of *transaction*—a ritual cleansing, a penalty-bearing, a reparation, or a conflation of these ideas. J. Denny Weaver rejects all notions of Christ's death as a payment or a satisfaction of the need for divine retribution.[60] Anselm's theory does reduce the idea of divine wrath, but:

> the death of Jesus is still directed Godward . . . . [saying that] It is God who has arranged the scenario that produced the Godward-directed death of Jesus in order to repay the honor of God. . . . All versions of satisfaction atonement, regardless of their packaging, assume the violence of retribution or justice based on punishment, and depend on God-induced and God-directed violence.[61]

But the moral influence theory is little better, since it "still leaves God the Father offering the Son's death to sinners as the example of

---

[59] Matt 7:9-11.
[60] J. Denny Weaver, "Violence in Christian Theology," in *Cross Currents* 51 (2001) 171.
[61] Ibid., 158.

Fatherly love."[62] The ideology of substitutionary atonement, by glorifying suffering and asking Christians to endure their suffering passively, allows people to be exploited.[63]

Weaver advocates the "narrative Christus Victor" interpretation of atonement since it involves no God-orchestrated death and no payment to God.[64] Since this model has Christ fighting the evil powers, the church also "confronts the world," remaining a nonviolent critic of the social order rather than accommodating itself to it.[65] The notion of the church "posing an alternative to the world disappears with the Constantinian synthesis,"[66] when Christianity became the imperial ideology. Further, this viewpoint forces us to "make use of the entire life and teachings of Jesus, rather than focus only on his death."[67]

While there is much to commend here, it says nothing about the biblical roots of atonement and offers little help in sorting out the differences between different biblical pictures of salvation. Further, this idea of a battle between cosmic forces of good and evil seems characteristic of the worldview of the first and second centuries and inadequate to answer our philosophic needs today. It does not present God as truly supreme, but as engaged in pitched battle with an evil force that is nearly God's equal. No great monotheistic philosopher, from Gregory of Nazianzus onward, could tolerate a God of such limited sovereignty.

Finally, it seems that Weaver is really describing *salvation* and *discipleship*, not *atonement* at all. He has spiritualized atonement completely out of the picture. While this may be a desirable destination, it is exegetically unsatisfying, and does not adequately account for the development of atonement doctrine in the first place. This kind of spiritualizing combines *rejectionist* and *reformist* views and operates by subverting traditional meanings of "atonement." But Christians will not simply forget what those meanings are; it is necessary to study their origin in—and their *alteration of*—biblical texts to see how they coordinate with other biblical teachings. More biblical basis is needed for any successful revision of atonement. One must use the Bible to critique the Bible.

In addition, Weaver's approach seems to come from a sectarian viewpoint: "The Christus Victor image of atonement assumes and reflects a

[62] Ibid., 162.
[63] Ibid., 163.
[64] Ibid., 172.
[65] Ibid., 170.
[66] J. Denny Weaver, "Atonement for the Nonconstantinian Church," in *Modern Theology* 6 (1989–90) 314.
[67] Weaver, "Violence," 171.

church over against the world."[68] But if there is only room for "Christ against culture" and none for "the Christ of culture,"[69] where is the place in Weaver's church for the faithful centurion, or for the wealthy father of a Prodigal Son, or for a vineyard owner, or a righteous tax collector? Jesus' parables are filled with salvageable characters that undermine all attempts to make any social group wholly negative—including the rich.

Of the pacifist-leaning theologians critical of atonement, Walter Wink does the best job of seeking a solid biblical grounding and showing just how the message of Jesus was distorted.

4.3.3 Wink: A Nearly Pacifist Gospel

Walter Wink articulates an understanding of the Gospel that is firmly committed to rejecting the violent way of the world represented by "the Domination System" and its ruling "Powers." He gives new meaning (or the old, original meaning?) to passages about the "world," as when he translates 1 John 5:19 like this: "The whole Domination System *(kosmos)* lies under the power of the Evil One."[70] Jesus repudiates the Powers and their favorite tool, violence. "By submitting to the authority of the Powers, Jesus acknowledged their necessity but rejected the legitimacy of their pretentious claims. He . . . de-absolutized, de-idolized them."[71]

Slavery to the Powers is largely an inward slavery. Some of the transcendent language of the ancient writers is really about the inner life. Wink finds "that 'the heavenlies' . . . are not off at the edge of space somewhere, but are in our very midst and the *interiority* of earthly institutions."[72] Jesus shows us the way to liberation from our internalized acceptance of violence as "normal. . . . Only those who have died to the Powers can make themselves expendable."[73] We recover our power when we refuse to fear the Powers, who, after all, are fear-dominated.

Wink makes a clear-headed distinction between the different views of atonement on offer in the NT and is able to say: "The early church was not able to sustain the intensity of this revelation"; they slid back

---

[68] Weaver, "Atonement," 319.

[69] H. Richard Niebuhr, *Christ and Culture* (New York: Harper & Row, 1951) 45–115.

[70] Walter Wink, *Engaging the Powers: Discernment and Resistance in a World of Domination* (Minneapolis: Fortress, 1992) 202.

[71] Wink, *Engaging*, 142.

[72] Ibid., 164.

[73] Ibid., 159, 163.

to the scapegoat idea, the "notion that God intended Jesus' death."[74] Jesus would tell people they were already forgiven (Mark 2:9), but early Christians resuscitated the God of "blood atonement" who requires a sacrificial death and who then "holds the whole of humanity accountable for a death that God both anticipated and required."[75] Wink recognizes that the "expiatory death of Jesus is far more pervasive in the New Testament than Girard acknowledges" and that Paul participates *both* in the expose of the scapegoating mechanism *and* in its re-inscription as a Christian doctrine, teaching that, "God caused Jesus to be a *final* 'sacrifice of atonement.'"[76]

Unfortunately, in summarizing Girard's view, Wink seems at one point to endorse its most problematic aspect, where Girard falls partly back into sacrificial thinking, saying that God allowed the killing of Jesus to actually function as a scapegoating act so that scapegoating might be exposed. The long history of human projection of violence onto God seems to be described here as part of God's plan: "The violence of the Bible is the necessary precondition for the gradual perception of the meaning of violence. . . . God was working through violence to expose violence for what it is and to reveal the divine nature as nonviolent."[77]

This is either a momentary lapse by Wink, or he is simply restating Girard's view. Jack Nelson-Pallmeyer assumes the former: "I find Wink's placement of the theory of scapegoating at the center of God's intent throughout scripture in conflict with his vital insight that Jesus reveals a nonviolent God. . . . A compassionate God is . . . incompatible with all atonement theories."[78]

Nelson-Pallmeyer is failing to appreciate that Wink shares his views, for "all such sacrifices are unnecessary," but "Paul has apparently been unable fully to distinguish the insight that Christ is the *end* of sacrificing from the idea that Christ is the *final* sacrifice whose death is an atonement to God. And Christianity has suffered from this confusion ever since."[79]

[74] Walter Wink, *The Powers That Be: Theology for a New Millennium* (New York: Doubleday, 1998) 87; cf. the nearly identical wording in idem, *Engaging,* 148.

[75] Wink, *Engaging,* 149; cf. idem, *Powers That Be,* 88–9.

[76] Wink, *Engaging,* 153; cf. idem, *Powers That Be,* 88.

[77] Wink, *Powers That Be,* 85–6.

[78] Jack Nelson-Pallmeyer, *Jesus Against Christianity: Reclaiming the Missing Jesus* (Harrisburg: Trinity, 2001) 222–4.

[79] Wink, *Powers That Be,* 88; idem, *Engaging,* 149, 153–4.

What do we make of Wink's social stance? He offers an apparently pacifist interpretation of the Gospel. The Gospel embraces the life of peace and mutuality, in opposition to all of society's violence. But he is inconsistent on particular cases. He says "Nonviolence *did* work whenever it was tried against the Nazis," and cites the example of the Bulgarian Orthodox Bishop who threatened a campaign of large-scale Christian and Jewish civil disobedience if Bulgaria's Jews were deported, and so saved Bulgaria's Jews, Wink says.[80] He goes on to cite many other examples, but he distorts the evidence, since he includes the Norwegian underground and the Italian resistance, without mentioning that they engaged in violent resistance. He asserts that "nonviolence did work when used against the Nazis,"[81] and implies that it should have been used consistently, across the board.

But he shatters the structure he has built when he goes on to give examples of justifiable violence against more recent regimes, like that of Nicaragua's Somoza: "When an oppressive regime has squandered every opportunity to do justice . . . violence . . . is a kind of apocalyptic judgment. In such a time, Christians have no business judging those who take up violence out of desperation."[82] How he decides that this regime was more intractable than the Nazis, I cannot fathom. He seems overly sympathetic to certain present-day liberation movements.

Wink is not unaware of dictatorial tendencies at both ends of the political spectrum. He includes, in his list of important non-violent actions, the Prague Spring activities of 1968,[83] though it would have been good also to include the human rights advocates in the USSR of the 1970s and 1980s. But he rightly states that "addict[ion] to violence . . . is as prevalent on the left as on the right,"[84] and he refers to "the slavery which communism imposed on a third of humanity."[85]

Wink courageously wrestles with a most thorny and complex problem. His solution may be the best one, but it would not be a strictly *pacifist* solution, when in fact he allows "*force*. . . . *Force* signifies a legitimate, socially authorized . . . use of restraint."[86] He allows that the

---

[80] Ibid., 153.
[81] Ibid., 158.
[82] Ibid., 159.
[83] Wink, *Engaging*, 247.
[84] Ibid., 202.
[85] Ibid., 166.
[86] Wink, *Powers That Be*, 159.

Powers do have some legitimacy. Thus, a blanket critique of the Powers turns out to have little analytical depth, and it is misleading when it presents itself as pacifism. One can hardly be partially pacifist any more than one can be partially pregnant. Wink's philosophy is not as fully worked out as he wants to imply. In fact, he is still wrestling with how people can properly respond to violent regimes—as we all are. When he says people can resort to force, he is not pacifist (as I understand the term). "Nonviolence" may be a better term, indicating a mode of social activism and a principled stance, but not meaning that force can never be used to defend a community. In sum, Wink is an important thinker, and more balanced than some others.

Liberation rhetoric is very common in the seminary business, but it should be questioned when it means the liberation of *some* groups at the expense of others. The conscious and deliberate politicization of the Gospel is a decadent and harmful choice that contributes to further polarization of opinion. Liberation theology of the partisan kind tries to sanctify its political slant by saying that the biblical message has always been directed to a particular human community. This is a backward glance. It is using the legitimate primitivism of the past to justify a retrograde motion in the present. The true direction of the Gospel (as of the progressive element in Judaism) is toward universalism: "to gather into one the dispersed children of God" (John 11:52); "many nations shall join themselves to the Lord on that day, and shall be my people" (Zech 2:11); "I am coming to gather all nations and tongues" (Isa 66:18).

We find Jesus resisting the political Messianism that his apostles insist on applying to him, even to the point of trying to make him king (John 6:15). He uses Psalm 110, where "David" calls the Messiah "lord," to challenge the very idea of Messiah as son of David (Mark 12:35-37). In Semitic cultures, no father would call his son "lord," therefore the lord-Messiah cannot be David's son. Jesus uses this fact as a crowbar to pry apart "Messiah" from the nationalistic attitudes wrapped up in the hope for a new "son of David." This categorical rejection of Davidic Messianism was too anti-traditional for his apostles to understand, and is still too antipolitical for many Christians to comprehend. The tyranny of politics—its suffocating rhetoric, its self-congratulating slogans, its enemy-bashing—is one of the things from which we need to be rescued.

4.3.4 *Feminist Rejection of a Gospel of Suffering*

One clear and effective critique of the traditional atonement doctrine that has made a real dent in the citadel of that doctrine is the
feminist critique originating in the 1970s. Joanne Carlson Brown and
Rebecca Parker wrote:

> The atonement [i]s the central reason for the oppressiveness of Chris-
> tianity. . . . Christianity is an abusive theology that glorifies suffer-
> ing. . . . We must do away with the atonement, this idea of a blood sin
> upon the whole human race . . . . this blood-thirsty God.[87]

This is a radical position and one motivated by worthy ethical concerns, but it is incorrect to identify "Christianity" with atonement, without remainder. Atonement is not an essential doctrine of Christianity but
is in fact derivative. The more central doctrine is the Incarnation (see
chapter 5). The Incarnation need not issue in the mythology of substitutionary atonement. God's participation in human life and God's in-
dwelling of Jesus of Nazareth in particular did not make the Crucifixion
inevitable or necessary. When Brown and Parker say that "Christianity is
at heart and essence justice, radical love, and liberation,"[88] this is inconsistent with their earlier identification of Christianity with atonement.

Brown's and Parker's humanitarian motives are clear: "Christian
theology with atonement at the center still encourages martyrdom and
victimization."[89] "Only if the church is the place where cycles of abuse
are named, condemned, and broken can it be a haven of blessing."[90]
"God . . . carrying out the suffering and death of his own son has sustained a culture of abuse."[91] But they do not fill this out with any biblical scholarship, any background in cultic theology or the
metaphorical appropriation of cultic images, or any history of the
phases of doctrinal development. Humanistic appeals are not enough
to provide the ground for a new theology. It is necessary to give a sustained account of how and why these doctrines emerged. Strong biblical scholarship is needed; the case against traditional atonement
cannot be argued with one's ethical instincts alone. Otherwise there is
little mooring or depth to one's attempted new theologizing.

---

[87] Brown and Parker, "For God So Loved," 26.
[88] Ibid., 27.
[89] Ibid., 3.
[90] Ibid., 4.
[91] Ibid., 9.

Let us look at Brown's and Parker's redefinition of redemption. They release the term from its original meaning: "Redemption happens when people refuse to relinquish respect and concern for others."[92] "'Suffering with' is itself a redeeming action."[93] But would such spiritualizing redefinitions flow forth so easily if the transactional background of *redemption* were explored? A term redolent of so much *specific* meaning cannot instantly be made to mean something else, unrelated. One could perhaps deliberately reverse its meaning, but one should at least demonstrate familiarity with its traditional meaning.

A more recent book that combines critical and traditional values is that of Cynthia Crysdale. Her approach combines psychology with Gospel: Jesus' forgiveness breaks the cycle of victimization. "The cycle sin-revenge-further violence was broken and the full possibility of human flourishing in union with God was met."[94] The new cycle is "healed-forgiven-healed."[95]

Crysdale wants "to retrieve a Christian faith with the cross and suffering front and center," even though she frankly acknowledges the fact of "'pathologies' of the cross."[96] She shares Wink's repudiation of the notion that God "rescued sinners by redemptive violence,"[97] and she recognizes the danger of "distorted spirituality—believers undertaking (deserved) suffering in order to please a sadistic God."[98]

However, she argues, suffering is the inevitable result of moral action when cruelty and violence reign; this is "suffering as a *consequence* of union with God, not the *means* to it."[99] "Suffering is not [a] value . . . [but] moral conversion . . . involves *accepting* suffering."[100] Those who endeavor to lift up and empower the downtrodden will experience retaliation, as Jesus did. "Authentic resistance thus becomes a statement of faith in eternal life."[101]

A similar point about suffering is made by Gorringe in his analysis of Jesus' words at the Last Supper. Is not Jesus speaking about self-sacrifice? Yes, says Gorringe, he is referring to the self-sacrifice that any committed

[92] Ibid., 19.
[93] Ibid., 16.
[94] Crysdale, *Embracing Travail*, 33.
[95] Ibid., 24.
[96] Ibid., xii.
[97] Ibid., 53.
[98] Ibid., 115.
[99] Ibid., 124.
[100] Ibid., 138.
[101] Ibid., 55.

person must undergo. Jesus anticipating his violent death "may have less to do with providence than with the fate of anyone who critiques the ruling powers."[102] Recognizing this ethical message of Jesus (nonviolence) enables the possibility of "a different, non-expiatory, account of the 'passion.'"[103] Any spiritual and courageous individual is going to find out what Jesus found out through bitter experience, that no prophet is without honor except in his own country and in his own family.

All of this raises the issue of God suffering, a popular idea now. What Berdyaev wrote fifty-five years ago is now standard fare: "Only God becoming man, taking upon himself the suffering of man and of all creation, can conquer the source of evil which engenders suffering."[104] God enters into the depths of human life, shares human suffering, and redeems evil by personally suffering it—notions that blend Christian principles with modern sensibilities. But this is ambiguous about whether God *intended* all this suffering and required some more of it from an innocent victim before salvation would be offered. In fact, its ambiguity is part of its appeal on the popular level.

I think the notion of God suffering can be a useful one, as long we are clear that God does not require blood sacrifice or payment. Rather, when we finally realize that God suffers silently, then the question of suffering ceases to be "how can you allow this?" and becomes: "how can you bear so much suffering, dear God, since you feel it *all*?" If we sense that God suffers the effects of evil, then we should feel moved to help God bear it, as well as to bring God's human race through its stormy youth, into better years. We must be willing to be heartbroken for God.

However, this may be a dangerous avenue for theologizing. The undertow of substitutionary thinking is very strong; it has drawn down many a brave swimmer. However, if we are aware of the religious currents upon which we swim, we should be able to find the current that leads to our destination.

4.4 Atonement: A Call for the Question

4.4.1 Is the Atonement Metaphor Inherently Flawed?

We may ask: is the cultic metaphor any worse than the metaphor about a "kingdom"? Let us consider two possible answers:

[102] Gorringe, *God's Just Vengeance*, 63.

[103] Ibid., 65.

[104] Nicolai Berdyaev, *Divine and the Human* (London: Geoffrey Bles, 1949), excerpted in *Christian Existentialism*, ed. Daniel Lowrie (New York: Harper & Row, 1965) 214.

(a) No, it is not. Jesus also used metaphors of God as a violent no-bleman[105] and as an unjust or grouchy judge,[106] but the rest of his teachings confirm rather the generosity[107] of God. The parables are not meant to teach systematic theology but a single, central point. For instance, the parable of the unjust or grouchy judge is meant to highlight "their need to pray always and not lose heart" (Luke 18:1), not to indicate that God is grouchy. The reasoning is this: if persistence can work even with a grouchy judge, *how much more* will it work with a just God? The parables are metaphors in story form; we do not take every element literally, nor should we take every element of Paul's metaphors literally. "Redemption" does not mean God actually paid anyone off, or paid Godself off; it just means God *rescued* people. Don't take the details of metaphors too literally; get the main point! Don't miss the forest (the *point*) for the trees (the *details*). Unless you want to condemn Jesus for his parable where the God-like figure, the nobleman, orders servants to be beaten, you cannot condemn Paul for a metaphor that merely implies that salvation followed upon a certain cultic significance to the death of Jesus.

(b) Yes, the cultic metaphor is harmful. One can have a good and just king, but not a good and just scapegoat ritual or human sacrifice. One can refrain from taking literally some secondary details in a parable, recognizing that they are there for rhetorical effect, but one cannot overlook the *main* implications of the sacrificial and scapegoat metaphors: that innocent blood purifies, or that God is moved by our ritual actions, or that the killing of Jesus was accepted as a payment for sins, apparently arranged by God: "the mystery that was kept secret" (Rom 16:25), "which God decreed before the ages for our glory" (1 Cor 2:7).[108] The Romans passage means *faith* was the thing kept secret and now revealed, but the Corinthians passage seems to mean the crucifying of the "Lord of glory" (2:8). In any case, many subsequent Christians assumed that the killing of the Messiah was a preordained plan. But many theists today can no longer accept the idea that God would not extend forgiveness and salvation until the rejection and killing of the divine Son should take place. Why could God not open up the way of salvation without a blood-rite? Is this not based on primitive beliefs about the polluting effect of sin and the magical cleansing power of lifeblood?

---

[105] Luke 12:42-48; 19:12-27.
[106] Luke 18:1-7.
[107] Matt 5:3-9; 6:20-21; 7:7-11; 9:12-13; Luke 10:21-37; 12:22-32; 15:1-32; 18:41-42.
[108] Cf. Eph 1:9-10; 3:9, 11, in what is possibly the earliest deutero-Pauline letter.

Frances Young laments the "polarization of opinion about atonement" and hopes that Christians can accept the idea that "the sacrifice of Christ was a sort of 'self-propitiation' offered by God to God to make atonement for the existence of evil in his universe. . . . God took responsibility for the existence of evil in his creation; he bore the pain of it."[109] While the latter idea has a certain appeal, the former suggestion—God's love offering a sacrifice to appease God's justice—is destructive of monotheism.

What security can there be in being saved by such a divided God? It echoes such notions as Luther's doctrine of "God against God":[110] a compassionate Son having to bargain with a stern and inscrutable Father, not the message that Jesus wanted to convey about "my Father and your Father" (John 20:17).

4.4.2 Can the Sacrifice Metaphor Be Spiritualized?

Can the sacrifice metaphor, in particular, be spiritualized? Can it be made useful? Does it say anything true about God?

(a) Yes, the whole history of sacrifice is one of constant spiritualization, first through substitution, then through reexplanation, then through insertion of ethics and heightened spirituality, then through its becoming a metaphor, so that people now *primarily* intend the metaphorical meaning when they say "sacrifice." Sacrifice *has* been so far spiritualized that it now means the best of human selflessness and dedication to a higher purpose. Jesus' life and death embodied selfless service to others. "Sacrifice" continues to call forth the best in people.

(b) No, that is, at least two aspects of sacrifice cannot be successfully spiritualized: its superstitious side (that innocent blood is purifying), and its bargaining side (that sacrifice is a payment that God honors). Continuing theologizing upon these bases perpetuates a terrifying and unjust God and will give rise to strange religious and political aberrations of violence and scapegoating.

In common usage, the term "sacrifice" has been so far spiritualized as to mean unselfish action accompanied with suffering, but in atonement theory it comes to mean "paying for" sin with a substitutionary death: a harmful idea that perpetuates a punishing and cruel mentality. Sacrifice as a way to win God's favor is manipulative. In both concept and feeling, this differs profoundly from what Jesus taught.

---

[109] Young, *Sacrifice*, 93–4.
[110] Gorringe, *God's Just Vengeance*, 134.

What, then, *did* Jesus say about his own impending death?

4.5 Did Jesus Have to Be Killed?

There are quite a few parables and remarks of Jesus that indicate that he did *not* think that it was God's will that he should be murdered.

In his parable of the vineyard, Jesus says the vineyard owner sent his son in order to "collect . . . his share of the produce of the vineyard" (Mark 12:2—a natural thing for a vineyard owner to do), not in order to have him be sacrificed or killed (a very *unnatural* thing for a father to do). The owner is not happy nor even sadly resigned when the tenants kill his son; he is angry. Clearly, this killing was not what he intended. The owner simply wanted a share of the produce. This theme of God wanting produce is neglected in the studies I have consulted, but it is fully consistent with Jesus' often-repeated stress on spiritual progress: the expectation that entrusted talents will yield a profit, the assumption that trees will bear fruit, the analogies of wheat or mustard growing,[111] and so on. What the owner wants from his vineyard is growth and prosperity. There is nothing here about sacrifice, about a life given in order to make satisfaction. Rather, we see themes that recur throughout the body of Jesus' teaching: God's legitimate expectation of loyalty and of spiritual produce from the covenant people and bitter disappointment over a violent and ignorant response.

Even despite the partial interest of two of the evangelists (Mark and John) in promoting doctrines of atonement, we find hardly a hint of atonement in their chronicling of Jesus' statements foretelling his death. Jesus says quite frankly that he is going to be killed and tries to prepare his apostles for the difficult experience that lies ahead for them.[112] Although the Gospels describe Jesus several times predicting his coming death (and although the evangelists have an interest in giving his death a saving significance), there is nothing to indicate that Jesus saw his own coming death as a cultic event. He simply did not preach a sacrificial theology.[113]

Jesus was not naïve about the "leaven of the scribes and Pharisees" and he dropped many biting remarks about it. "It is impossible for a prophet to be killed outside of Jerusalem" (Luke 13:33) is a sarcastic comment about the cruelty and narrow-mindedness of the priestly

---

[111] Luke 19:22-26; Matt 7:17-20; Mark 11:20-22; 4:28-32.
[112] Matt 16:21-26; 17:22; 20:17-19; Mark 13:9-15.
[113] Girard, *Things Hidden*, 180–3, 187–8, 213.

leadership, not about what *God* requires. "The Son of Man is to be betrayed into human hands, and they will kill him" (Mark 9:31) is a statement about *human beings*, not about God. The next statement, that "he will rise again," speaks of the Divine.

When he wanted to spell out his mission, Jesus chose the universalizing and healing message of Isaiah 61, "to bring good news to the poor . . . release to the captives and recovery of sight to the blind."[114] But humanity was not prepared to accept this Isaianic mission of Jesus, and instead, they imposed upon him the tragic narrative of Isaiah 53, the rejecting, the wounding, the pouring out of his life (Isa 53:3, 5, 12). Even Paul said that if the "rulers of this age" had known "God's wisdom, secret and hidden, which God decreed before the ages . . . . they would not have crucified the Lord of glory" (1 Cor 2:7-8).

And the end of his career, Jesus makes it clear that he had hoped to take Jerusalem under his wing as a hen takes its chicks; he mourns for this city that kills its prophets (Matt 23:34, 37), which is not what God intends. Jesus would have taught them, would have led them into a new age where they would become a magnet for Gentile truth seekers, as envisioned by Isaiah and his tradents (those who hand on a tradition).[115]

Jesus did not come to earth in order to be murdered. He tried to lead his people into a new age of spiritual illumination, which would have followed upon acceptance of his revelation. The great unfulfilled prophecy remains the one Jesus used to identify his mission: to proclaim liberty to the spiritual prisoners, to open the eyes of the blind, to extend salvation to the ends of the earth.

The Cross symbolizes two very common human evils: the cruelty of the state and the violent envy of religious hierarchies. It also symbolizes God's involvement in the human predicament, God's willingness to go the full measure of participation in human suffering. But it is an error to describe all this as God's will. Some pain will always attend human growth, but the oppression of the innocent, the persecution of truth-tellers, is not God's will and will not go on forever. Someday "the earth will be filled with the knowledge of the glory of the Lord, as the waters cover the sea" (Isa 11:9; Hab 2:14).

What *did* Jesus teach, particularly as regards the connection with God?

---

[114] Luke 4:18; he is quoting Isa 61:1; 42:7; 58:6.
[115] Isa 2:2-3; 42:6-7; 49:6; 66:23; cf. John 9:5; Luke 2:32; Acts 13:47; 26:23; Jesus taught in Phoenicia (Mark 7:24, 31) and had Greek followers (John 12:20).

4.6 The Soteriology of Jesus

In Jesus' teachings as they are recorded in the canon, the way to God is *already open*. We have seen that Jesus *six times* tells people, "your faith has saved you,"[116] using the perfect tense, indicating that the action happened in the past and that its results continue in the present. Jesus is telling these people that their faith has *already* saved them (or *healed* them[117]). And again, despite the theological influence of atonement thinking, we find no mention of a sacrificial death. Jesus does not say, "your faith has saved you, contingent upon your accepting a soon-to-come interpretation of my death as a cosmic cleansing, a penal substitution, or a massive ransom payment." Rather, faith allows people to be saved because it allows God to reach into their lives and heal them. (Of course, it is God doing the actual saving.)

People who had dealings with Jesus knew that God was *already* saving people. One needs "no sacrificial intermediary"[118] with the heavenly Father. What is advised in the sunlight of such a God is open-hearted trust: "Do not be afraid, little flock, for it is your Father's good pleasure to give you the kingdom" (Luke 12:32). Obviously, this is a very different father from the fathers with whom many people grew up.

Salvation requires only a right attitude—or rather a right *hunger*: "Blessed are those who hunger and thirst for righteousness, for they will be filled" (Matt 5:6). A true disciple must trust that the Father wants to given him good things (bread, not a stone; Matt 7:9). There is no need to bargain with such a God, "for the Father himself loves you" (John 16:27).

Faith itself is life-giving, even healing, nor should this be called "Pelagian."[119] It is false humility to condemn the notion of immediate access to God as being insufficiently dependent upon the grace of God. On the contrary, those who use "Pelagian" as a bludgeon against the pure in heart have obscured and blocked the grace of God by hedging salvation about with doctrinal complexities and clerical authority. It was Jesus who said, "be perfect, therefore, as your heavenly Father is perfect" (Matt 5:48), and it is improper for us to throw out this straightforward message of the Savior in favor of convoluted and pessimistic doctrines.

---

[116] Luke 7:50; 8:48; 17:19; 18:42; Mark 5:34; 10:52.

[117] *Sesōken* is the perfect tense form of the Greek verb *sōzō*, meaning "has saved," "has healed," or "has rescued." NRSV assumes healing or "making well" in four of these passages, using "saved" only in Luke 7:50; 18:42. NAB reads healing in four passages, using "has been your salvation" in Luke 7:50; 17:19.

[118] Girard, *Things Hidden*, 183.

[119] The label comes from Augustine's opposition to Pelagius for supposedly teaching salvation by "works."

The teaching of trust was faithfully recorded in the Gospels as the core of the message of Jesus, but it did not become the core of the Christian Gospel, which has much more of a traumatic and dramatic basis, and is articulated in the epistles. God as *"your* Father"[120] is virtually the identifying mark of the dominical tradition, but was de-emphasized by Christianity, which focused instead on God as *Jesus'* Father and on the judgment facing each soul. One manifestation of this different mentality is seen in the different attitude toward ritual purity.

4.6.1 The Hosea Principle

To really understand Christ's life mission it is necessary to discard sacrificial thinking. God has said (and Hosea and Jesus are our witnesses) "I desire steadfast love and not sacrifice" (Hos 6:6). Jesus uses this saying to combat the tendency to rate purity laws more highly than persons, even persons who are doing God's work. Jesus points out the linkage between ritual fastidiousness, and violence against prophets: "If you had known what this means, 'I desire mercy and not sacrifice,' you would not have condemned the guiltless" (Matt 12:7).

It is precisely those with poor spiritual discernment, who fail to choose mercy over sacrifice, and so harm "the guiltless." Whenever we fail to understand the Hosea principle, we place ritual minutiae above persons, and we commit injustice. The first requirement is to understand that God does not require sacrificial payment but rather love and justice. Believers and scholars alike have been unwilling to accept this simple and straightforward dominical teaching. Naturally, then, they have not comprehended the appended teaching: that violence derives from failure to grasp such spiritual fundamentals as the generosity of God and the fact that there really are "guiltless" people!

According to Mark, Jesus defends his followers gleaning grain on the Sabbath by comparing them to priests and to the followers of David, and climaxes with a stunning affirmation of the value of humanity over holy days: "The sabbath was made for humankind, and not humankind for the sabbath" (2:27), while Matthew has him affirming that "something greater than the temple is here" (12:6)—a shocking remark in a temple-centered society.

In these sayings, Jesus stresses the anti-cultic, the "not sacrifice" half of Hosea's saying. In Matthew 9:13 he emphasizes the "steadfast love (*ḥesed*)" half of the saying: When Jesus responds to the criticism that

---

[120] Matt 5:48; ten times in ch. 6; 7:11; etc.; Mark 11:25; Luke 6:36; 12:30; John 20:17.

his followers eat with tax collectors and sinners, he points out that he came to heal the *needy* (those who "need a physician," the "sick," the "sinners": Mark 2:17; Matt 9:12-13). This is a compassionate message, more inclusive than any purity code would allow. In the middle of this response is where Matthew places Jesus' exhortation that they "go and learn what this means, 'I desire mercy, not sacrifice.'" Here the Hosea principle is interpreted as compassion for the needy, kindness instead of ritual fastidiousness. Jesus certainly contrasted inward purity with ritual purity (Matt 15:11-20; 23:23-28).[121]

The next story, in both Matthew and Mark, is where Jesus warns the disciples of John against trying to pour new wine into old wineskins: trying to confine new truth in old ways of thinking. The new wine of Jesus cannot be poured into the old skins of ritualistic religion. The Pharisaic concern with external ritual correctness (on the Sabbath and at the dining table) is replaced with the Hosea principle of compassion embodied in Jesus' ministry to the needy, to those who are paralyzed by sin or withered by misfortune. The message is: God is pouring out new wine, and it leads to goodness and kindness, but will have to come into conflict with old ritualistic ways of thinking.

4.6.2 Jesus at Odds with Ritual Correctness

Jesus' focus often puts him at odds with cultic concerns. For instance, he wants the Temple to be a "house of prayer for all nations" (Mark 11:17); his concern is not cultic (*contra* Chilton[122]), if it were, he would have demanded the exclusion of foreigners who only *increase* impurity from the cultic point of view. Cultic concerns are linked with ethnic barriers but the dominical sayings call ethnic barriers into question. Even when Jesus tells someone to bring an offering to the altar (a ritual act), his point is that if one has something against one's brother (a moral problem), one should immediately stop the ritual and "go; first be reconciled to your brother"; only then may one finish the ritual (Matt 5:24). This passage shows Jesus did not rigidly oppose the cultic system, but we must not overlook its main point: reconciliation happens through interpersonal, not ritual, means. Reconciliation must be

---

[121] James D. G. Dunn, *Jesus, Paul, and the Law: Studies in Mark and Galatians* (Louisville, Ky.: Westminster, 1990) 52–3. John Riches goes further, saying Jesus rejected the purity system (*Jesus and the Transformation of Judaism* [New York: Seabury, 1980] 142–4).

[122] Bruce Chilton, *The Temple of Jesus: His Sacrificial Program within a Cultural History of Sacrifice* (University Park: Pennsylvania State University Press, 1992) 134–6.

attended to first; cult may have some secondary importance, but it is less important than the interpersonal matter.

What of the Gospels' institution passages, where his blood acts like covenant sacrificial blood? It is important to note that these are the *only* places in the Gospels where blood-atonement occurs. This fact alone ought to alert students to be suspicious of their historicity. In fact, these texts early came under pressure to conform to standard liturgical usage.[123] The widespread disagreements in Luke manuscripts over the presence, the wording, and the order of the "body . . . blood" passage (Luke 22:19b-20) shows there was quite a debate over this text. These verses are simply absent from the oldest Western Greek manuscript (D) and from the oldest Latin and Syriac versions, suggesting the possibility that they were added to Luke at some point, fairly early on.[124] The verses *are* present in most Greek manuscripts but with numerous variations in verse ordering and with some added phrases.[125] With good reason, the REB translation drops the "body-blood" passage from Luke altogether, leaving us with no cultic theology but only a touching farewell scene where Christ says he will not again share the fruit of the vine with his friends until he shares it in the kingdom of God, something that is surely more consistent with the rest of the dominical teaching than is any kind of cultic theology.

The cultic concept is the central metaphor of salvation in Revelation and the epistles (except in James, Second Peter, and Jude) but is nearly absent from the Gospels and can with confidence be said to be alien to the teachings of Jesus, for whom salvation and wholeness are freely available without any mediating *transaction*, for whom faith means trusting in God's straightforward generosity, and for whom forgiveness is conditioned only by one's willingness to forgive others.

We see a completely different attitude in the Fourth Gospel and in Paul where Jesus is the fulfillment of the Jewish festivals and institutions, which are types. In John, Jesus fulfills the symbolism of several Jewish festivals, while in Paul he becomes the true *hilastērion*, the sin-sacrifice, the second Adam. For the Fourth Gospel and Paul, there is not the same contrast between ritual and compassion that one sees in the Synoptics.

---

[123] Bart D. Ehrman, "The Cup, The Bread, and the Salvific Effect of Jesus' Death in Luke-Acts," *SBLSP* 1991, ed. Eugene H. Lovering Jr. (Atlanta: Scholars, 1991) 577–8, 591.

[124] Christopher F. Evans, *Saint Luke* (London: SCM, 1990) 787–9. But many disagree, such as N. T. Wright, *Jesus and the Victory of God* (Minneapolis: Fortress, 1996) 560 n. 85.

[125] Joseph A. Fitzmyer, *The Gospel According to Luke [X–XXIV]*, AB 28A (Garden City, N.Y.: Doubleday, 1985) 1387.

But the Gospels show that this conflict between Jesus' teaching and the ritualistic emphasis of the religious professionals of his day was central to the outcome of the story. It was the advocates of ritual correctness (the Pharisees) and the landlords of ritual sacrifice (the Sadducees) who orchestrated Jesus' death, and, further, their ritualistic attitudes were linked to their hostile actions.[126] The message of this boundary-breaking Galilean prophet concerned them and threatened them far more than it posed any threat to the Romans who were usually perceptive regarding the insurrectionary potential (or lack thereof) of local religious movements. The Jewish religious establishment wanted Jesus killed and coerced a weak-willed Roman procurator into carrying it out. Jesus was no threat to the Romans, but he was a real threat to the religious class structure of Jewish society.

Facing the facts about Jewish involvement in the killing of Jesus is not anti-Semitic. Anti-Semitism has two main causes; one is historical and ideological: the intellectual hostility that inevitably emerges when communities separate over religious issues. This gave rise to bitter condemnations by both sides. The other cause is the one that produces violence: when Christians take on envy, greed, and the habit of projecting undesirable qualities onto the "other"; this is the scapegoating mob that Girard describes. These anti-Semites most closely resemble the people who killed Jesus.

But there is a unique Christian psychology of anti-Semitism. In the unconscious mind of a Christian, a Jew is a symbolic Christian. The Jew therefore becomes the preferred target for a Christian to project all of his distress about his own religion, distress that is largely the product of crude atonement doctrines. This practice of projecting one's self-loathing and distress onto others is called "projective inversion," a psychological mechanism that can be seen throughout Christian history, but which is particularly obvious in the details of the medieval blood-libel legend. Christian anxiety about eating the Lord's body and drinking his blood was projected outward, leading to the accusation against Jews of drinking the blood of Christian children.[127] When the atonement doctrine was taken most literally by Christians, with promulgation of

---

[126] Because of his neglect of ritual washing and after his scathing critique of their ritualism, the Pharisees begin to plot against him (Luke 11:37-54), while, for the priests, Jesus' Temple critique was among the principal accusations against him (Mark 14:55-60).

[127] Alan Dundes, "The Ritual Murder or Blood Libel Legend: A Study of Anti-Semitic Victimization through Projective Inversion," in *The Blood Libel Legend: A Casebook in Anti-Semitic Folklore* (Madison: University of Wisconsin Press, 1989) 344, 354–8, 366.

the doctrine of transubstantiation in 1215, anti-Semitism experienced a sharp increase.

The atonement doctrine is a font of anti-Semitism, not through the malice of the founders of Christianity, and certainly not of Paul, but because of the dark and frightening logic wrapped up in violent cult, and even in spiritualizing metaphors based on it. The metaphors themselves carry harmful implications, at least for those who take them literally, and Christians in the Middle Ages took them very literally. The notion of a violent God fuels the tendency to find human scapegoats.

Regarding the phenomenon of projective inversion, Freud recognized it in Nazism. Observing Nazi hostility to Christianity and the more openly expressed hostility to Judaism, he remarked, "The hatred for Judaism is at bottom hatred for Christianity."[128]

It is important for us to notice, though, that atonement is intertwined with many important and essential Christian teachings such as the compassion of God, the fact of the divine Incarnation, and the certainty of eventual vindication of the just. Many people instinctively fear the loss of these beliefs if atonement is surrendered.

---

[128] Sigmund Freud, *Moses and Monotheism*, 145; quoted in Nicholas Berdyaev, *Christianity and Anti-Semitism* (New York: Philosophical Library, 1954) 53.

The Incarnation

5.1 The Incarnation Interpreted through Secondary Doctrines

The central doctrine that is unique to Christianity is the Incarnation, the teaching about the enfleshed Word, the sent Son, the temporarily God-emptied Messiah.[1]

The Christian idea of Incarnation is not a repetition of Greek notions of the gods appearing in human form. It is closer to the Jewish idea of Wisdom as God's agent or emanation. Christ or the Logos is he through whom "all things in heaven and on earth were created,"[2] even "the worlds,"[3] and who is a heavenly ruler,[4] "emptying" himself and taking on human form (Phil 2:7). Since his children were flesh and blood, he took on flesh and blood, becoming like mortals "in every respect" (Heb 2:14, 17), tested as mortals are (Heb 4:15). This God-man,[5] this divine mortal,[6] is able to sympathize with frail humans, "to deal gently with the ignorant and wayward, since he himself is subject to weakness" (Heb 5:2). Christianity wrestled with this extraordinary idea for over four hundred years, culminating in the formula uttered at the Council of Chalcedon in 451, that Christ was fully human *and* fully divine, something that could not be said about any other person.

This was the unique and difficult doctrine over which Christianity had to obsess for centuries or lose its unique revelation. Unfortunately, reflection was accompanied by political factors: increasing clerical and

---

[1] John 1:14; Gal 4:4; Phil 2:7.
[2] Col 1:16-17; cf. John 1:3, 10; 1 Cor 8:6.
[3] Heb 1:2; 11:3.
[4] Matt 28:18; 1 Cor 15:27; Phil 2:9; Eph 1:20-23; 4:10; Col 2:15; Heb 1:4.
[5] Used by many Eastern Orthodox writers, apparently first expressed by Origen.
[6] A phrase of my friend Sue Wilson-Pettit.

doctrinal control, and an intense pressure to conform placed on the average believer. The episcopal and imperial power structures asserted control, tending to shut down theological inquiry. However, the notion of the Incarnation has biblical roots; it does not derive from—though it was used by—the political church.

This is an example of something that can be seen happening on many different levels in the Christian world: something original and essential (the doctrine of the Incarnation) gets surrounded by secondary elements (the political church). We see this happening from the very beginning, within the NT period itself, with the atonement doctrine (a secondary development) attaching itself to the primary idea (the Incarnation). It is not surprising that a unique idea should become assimilated to, and absorbed by, existing beliefs. Every religious reformer's ideas get adapted and assimilated to existing religious practice. The words of fiery ethical teachers, critical of ritual and priestly control, are used in the priestly rituals of later generations. Jesus mocks those who wear soft robes and live in palaces (Matt 11:8), and these words are then bound in gold-covered Bibles and carried about by soft-robed priests, sometimes in rituals conducted in palaces. To show that my point is not about *wealth* but about *adaptation* and *assimilation* I give an ascetic example: Jesus feasts and drinks wine with his friends, but ascetics come to dominate Christianity. The asceticizing of Christianity was an adaptation to a widespread trend in Hellenistic religions (and also reflected in the Jewish *Testaments of the Twelve Patriarchs*) toward renunciation of the flesh.

Atonement, too, was a common category of religious belief. Atonement is not unique to Christianity. It was able to catch on in Christianity because it drew upon a pool of ideas common to the religions of the region. Even today we see atonement ideas (as well as ideas of hell) in Buddhism, Islam, and other religions, particularly in the common people's beliefs.

When the Incarnation gets attached to old notions of punishment, a collective stain of sin, and God responding to ritual, then the Incarnation gets taken over by concepts of atonement. The secondary beliefs are common, are accessible to more people, and so they absorb and dominate the more original, but difficult to understand, idea. This happens from the very beginning with the Incarnation. We saw that the Epistle to the Hebrews stresses that the Incarnated Son became vulnerable like other humans; but Hebrews also wraps this incarnational idea up with a familiar image: the high priest.

One element of the Incarnation is the divinity of Jesus. For many believers today, and for the authors of the nativity narratives in Matthew and Luke, the divinity of Jesus gets communicated through the secondary doctrine of the virginity of Mary. Divinity, when interpreted by minds that believe that the flesh is wholly corrupt, has to be sharply separated from the sinful flesh. Only by having a virginal conception, by having no relation to human lust, could Christ be truly divine. For many people today, the proof of the divinity of Jesus is in his alleged miraculous birth. But the essential idea is really the divinity of Jesus, not the mythological notion that is used to communicate it. The mythology is a vehicle. When the mythology fades, the original notion can be restated in ways that are closer to the original concept, but many believers cannot discard the "old wineskin," cannot see that it was just a vessel to convey something.

Likewise, the ritual bases upon which the mythology of substitutionary atonement is constructed (sacrifice and scapegoat) are no longer practiced. What would happen if we spoke about the heroic suffering of Jesus, his comprehension of what it was like to be human, but discarded the notion that God would not grant forgiveness to humanity until the Innocent One was killed? What happens if we restate the divine Incarnation of Jesus, thereby highlighting the fact of God's near approach to humanity and to human suffering through the Incarnation of Jesus through his *whole* life, but drop the idea of any magical transaction taking place at the cross?—What happens is that we return to Jesus' parental God who wants only spiritual progress and maturation for God's offspring. But then we may also meet with the anger of a religious mob like the one that took offense at Stephen's remark, "the Most High does not dwell in houses made with human hands" (Acts 7:48).

Detaching the Incarnation from ancient superstitions about sacrificial obeisance, patronage, ritual magic, and retribution enables us to more clearly discern the ethical and spiritual content of Jesus' life and teachings; for instance, his dissent from all abusive psychology and authority. Jesus neither taught an abusive God-concept nor, when he was being railroaded toward the cross, did he engage in self-blame, as many victims do. He rejected the whole mythology of sacrifice.

Now, if one decides that the death of Jesus was not a divinely planned ritual event, one still needs to say what his death *does* mean, but one is forced to do so without magical categories of thinking. We are moved to recognize some all-too familiar patterns: it was the cynical politics of turf protection that led to the plot against Jesus due to his exposing the exploitativeness and hypocrisy of the religious leadership in his society.

The Incarnation is an essential Christian idea; the Atonement—at least one that entails God as Sacrifice Demander and Jesus as punishment-bearer—is not. It is a mistake to identify atonement as the central Christian doctrine, although it is central to the Pauline tradition, to First Peter, Hebrews, First John, and Revelation. But these books, in their entirety, compose only 39 percent of the NT. The main positive function of atonement doctrine has been to help transmit information about the Incarnation of the divine Son. But that information can be transmitted just as well without atonement, as is seen in the Gospels and Acts of the Apostles.

I know many Christians will point out that if we let go of the atonement, we may also start letting go of other beliefs like christology and the Incarnation. We see this, for instance, in Brown's and Parker's remark that "Jesus is one manifestation of Immanuel but not uniquely so."[7] It may have partially been to guard against such views as this that Christians developed doctrines meant to tie down and secure the divinity of Jesus: the virginal conception, the "precious blood" (1 Pet 1:19), and other such notions derived from ancient realms of religious thought. However, such primitive mythology is no longer convincing for many people.

We need to reexplore the subject of the Incarnation and see if we can find more enlightened ways of comprehending and explaining it so that we can address the problem of decadent christology. If we can communicate the Gospel without violent metaphors, there may be people who will receive this message with joy, whose faith will be reborn.

Atonement has always been a vehicle for conveying information about salvation and the Incarnation. But there are other vehicles, and the best one might be a very old one.

5.2 *Theōsis*

Some interpretations focus on the fact of God incarnating in flesh, and so on the saving effect of the *life* of Jesus. These approaches often coincide with the important early Christian doctrine of *theōsis* preserved by Eastern Orthodoxy and now being gradually rediscovered

---

[7] Brown and Parker, "For God So Loved," 27, borrowing the idea from Dorothy Soelle.

by Western theology. This is the notion, well expressed by Irenaeus, that, "Jesus Christ became what we are in order that we might become what he himself is."[8] This is a concept of salvation history "culminating in the deification of believing humanity."[9] The Son came to rescue, even to re-divinize, human nature. By coming into a human body, God has permeated *human life*, and this creates a potential for spiritualizing[10] the race. This is part of Irenaeus's theory of "recapitulation" that states that Christ recapitulated human life in himself, living through, and sanctifying, each stage of human life.[11] Recapitulation means that the divine Son salvaged each phase of human life by his living through it. The *living* of this life had the effect of remaking human life itself, of restoring the potential for union with God.

Although Irenaeus plugs transactional terms like ransom,[12] propitiation,[13] and redemption[14] into this framework, they mainly describe the problem; they do not provide the content of the recapitulation idea. Not atonement, but *restoration* and *re-enabled participation in divinity* are the pillars of recapitulation. Irenaeus reasons that it was necessary for God to become human and to slay sin so that it would be a *human* who was slaying sin, but this is just part of a controlling concept of rescue and restoration. The goal for humans is participation in the divine: as he goes on to say in that section, the only way that humanity might "participate in incorruption" is by being "united with God."[15]

The fundamental insight of *theōsis* is simple but profound: "The Word . . . became man so that you might learn from man how man may become God."[16] God's will is the knowledge of God;[17] which is certainly a biblical theme. On balance, though, Christian *theōsis* ideas do seem to add some of Plato ("to become like God, to become righteous and holy and wise"[18]) to the teachings of Jesus and Paul. It seems overly fastidious to try to banish all Platonic thought from Christian

---

[8] *Adv. Haer.* 5, preface; from Harnack, *History of Dogma*, II:288.

[9] Harnack, *History of Dogma*, II:244.

[10] This is "Level Six spiritualizing," which means making-spiritual, making-holy, -good, -true.

[11] *Adv. Haer.* 3.18.1, 7; 2.22.4; Kelly, *Early Christian*, 173.

[12] *Adv. Haer.* 5.1.1.

[13] *Adv. Haer.* 5.17.1.

[14] *Adv. Haer.* 4.5.4; Kelly, *Early Christian*, 174.

[15] *Adv. Haer.* 3.19.6; Rashdall, *Idea of the Atonement*, 239.

[16] Clement of Alexandria, *Protre.* 1.8.4; Kelly, *Early Christian*, 184.

[17] Clement of Alexandria, *Strom.* 4.6.27.

[18] *Theaetatus* 176B, from *Plato*, vol. 2, trans. H. N. Fowler. LCL (London: Wm. Heinemann, 1921) 129.

theology.[19] Many early Christians saw Plato as a prophet to the Gentiles. His hopes and values, transformed by biblical monotheism, made a contribution to Christian theology, and that should no more be a matter of embarrassment than should the presence of foreign Magi at the nativity scene. The key Christian teachings on *theōsis* and on every other topic are biblical.

The important fourth-century theologian and bishop Athanasius of Alexandria emphasizes divinization: "The Word became man so that we might be deified."[20] Human *theōsis* derives from the divinizing work Christ did while in the flesh. We see this again in Gregory of Nyssa's notion of "the birth of God in humanity . . . . in order that our nature, by this admixture with the divine, should itself become divine."[21] Here a doctrine about Christ (Incarnation) drives a teaching about God's work in us (being made divine) and our work in the world (to make it divine).

We encounter such ideas again and again among the Greek (and Greek-writing) fathers of the church in its first several centuries, but they are also found in Latin and Reformed theology, despite the dominance of legalistic interpretations. Augustine allows that God can "deify a mere mortal,"[22] and "wants to make you a god . . . by adoption."[23] Calvin, although more known for his views on predestination and the total depravity of man, also can speak of "a kind of deification. . . . When we have put off all the vices of the flesh we shall be partakers of divine immortality and the glory of blessedness."[24]

Theōsis has a biblical basis, and this should not be forgotten. There is the promise that "you may become participants of the divine nature" (2 Pet 1:4); there is the command to become perfect, Godlike (Matt 5:48); there are the prophecies of doing greater things than Jesus

---

[19] N. T. Wright condemns "unwarranted platonizing of Christian hope" (*The Resurrection of the Son of God* [Minneapolis: Fortress, 2003] 367), equating Plato only with escapism (355), overlooking his actual focus on social responsibility and ethics.

[20] *De incarn.* 54; Kelly, *Early Christian*, 378.

[21] *Or. Catech.* 25; Henry Bettenson, ed., *The Later Christian Fathers: A Selection from the Writings of the Fathers from St. Cyril of Jerusalem to St. Leo the Great* (Oxford: Oxford University Press, 1970) 134.

[22] *Enarrat. Ps.* 117.11; *Expositions of the Psalms (99–120); The Works of Saint Augustine: A Translation for the 21st Century*, vol. III/19, tr. Maria Boulding (Hyde Park, N.Y.: New City Press, 2003) 337. The reference is from Robert Puchniak, "Augustine's Conception of Deification Revisited," to be published in *Theōsis: Deification in Christian Theology* (Wipf & Stock, 2005).

[23] *Serm.* 166.4; *Sermons (148–183) On The New Testament. The Works* (same series), vol. III/5, trans. Edmund Hill (1992) 209.

[24] *Calvin's New Testament Commentaries. Vol. 12: Hebrews and 1 and 2 Peter*, trans. W. B. Johnston, ed. D. W. and T. F. Torrance (Grand Rapids, Mich.: Eerdmans, 1963) 330.

did (John 14:12) and of revelations yet to be seen (John 1:51). *Theōsis* means each person incarnating divinity in his or her small way, inspired by the direct Incarnation of divinity that took place in Galilee and Judea. There is actually a kind of change of nature: "All of us, with unveiled faces, seeing the glory of the Lord as though reflected in a mirror, are being transformed into the same image from one degree of glory to another; for this comes from the Lord, the Spirit" (2 Cor 3:18). We are supposed to share in the life of God: "As you, Father, are in me and I am in you, may they also be in us" (John 17:20).

Theōsis connects with the notion of progressive, step-by-step development. None of the church fathers who writes about divinization claims to have achieved it. Obviously, its fulfillment lies in the afterlife, but its beginning is in this life, and the suppression of this teaching has been costly to Western Christianity. *Theōsis* stands at the pinnacle of a mature religious philosophy that takes seriously the human tasks of improvement in ethics, family life, and adjudication between nations, but recognizes that none of these, by itself, is the whole of the human task. Divinization or *theōsis* is the sum and goal of all worthwhile endeavor: "Mankind has to *co-operate* with God in this work, for otherwise there cannot be a complete oneing of God with his creatures and a full expression of the meaning of existence."[25] We can become *allies with God*, assisting the work that Jesus said he came to initiate: "I came not to judge the world, but to save the world" (John 12:47). "The Son of Man came to seek out and to save the lost" (Luke 19:10).

The great problem with humanity is its immaturity. Sin and violence are a huge part of the problem, but so are confusion, superstition, illiteracy, disease, pollution, political corruption, and inadequate philosophy. We need progress in all areas of human life but especially in receptivity to truth about the parental love of God, slowly moving humanity toward that day when, finally, "God [will] be all in all" (1 Cor 15:28). "We must grow up in every way into him who is the head, into Christ" (Eph 4:15). As Paul taught, believers are "transformed" (Rom 2:12), "made new" (2 Cor 5:17; Col 3:10), actually taking on "the mind of Christ" (1 Cor 2:16; Phil 2:5).

Whether or not one wishes to utilize the terminology of *theōsis*, which is still a strange and threatening concept to many Western Christians, there are many ways to return to the concept of the Incarnation without investing all of its significance in the death and turning the life into nothing but a lengthy prologue. No! This was the divine

---

[25] Soloviev, *God, Man and the Church*, 134.

life "come down from heaven" (John 6:50); the divine in the human *is* "the bread of life" (6:48). We need to learn from the whole of Jesus' life, including the death.

In his clearest statement about his life purpose, Jesus says that his purpose is to reveal truth: "For this I was born, and for this I came into the world, to testify to the truth" (John 18:37). And if "the truth will make you free"(John 8:32), then freedom seems to be part of Jesus' plan for the human race, but so also is spiritual unity: "that they may become completely one, so that the world may know that you have sent me" (John 17:23). Freedom and unity have often seemed, in both political and religious affairs, to be impossible to reconcile, but real ethical progress has only happened when and where some progress has been made in balancing and preserving freedom with unity.

Truth, honestly received, is liberating. Freedom, responsibly borne, leads to maturity. Maturity with freedom enables the overcoming of selfish and narrow loyalties, and that enables the possibility of unity. "Unity of the faith" is a logical byproduct of "knowledge of the Son," of "maturity," and of growing up into "the full stature of Christ" (Eph 4:13).

True freedom is not anarchic. It does not free one from one's obligations to others, including the most important Other. Rather, freedom means outgrowing the doctrines of an arbitrary and punishing God, accepting a more mature concept of the Divine Parent who is most interested in our growth, even in the transformation of God's children "from one degree of glory to another" (2 Cor 3:18). Even if we do not wish to use the *theōsis* concept, we need to recognize that God's interest is in fostering spiritual growth and ethical progress. God does not need sacrifice or payment, any more than any loving parent does. A parent only wants to see some "produce" (Mark 12:2)—some spiritual growth!

Bibliography

Primary Sources (and for which language):

Abelard (English): E. R. Fairweather, editor and translator. *A Scholastic Miscellany*. London: SCM, 1956.

Athanasius (English): *On the Incarnation*. Edited and translated by a Religious of C.S.M.V. Crestwood, N.Y.: St. Vladimir's Seminary Press, 1998.

Augustine. Two English volumes used:

Sermons (94A–147A). The Works of Saint Augustine: A Translation for the 21st Century, vol. III/4. Translated by Edmund Hill, O.P., 1992.

Sermons (148–183) On The New Testament. The Works [same series as above], vol. III/5. Translated by Edmund Hill, O.P., 1992.

Barnabas (English): *The Didache, the Epistle of Barnabas, the Epistles and Martyrdom of St. Polycarp, the Fragments of Papias, the Epistle to Diognetus*. Translated by James A. Kleist. Ancient Christian Writers: the Works of the Fathers in Translation 6. New York and Mahwah: Paulist, 1948.

The Bible (English): New Revised Standard Version (NRSV), unless otherwise indicated.

Calvin, Jean. Two English sources used:

Calvin's New Testament Commentaries. Vol. 12: Hebrews and 1 and 2 Peter. Translated by W. B. Johnston. Edited by D. W. and T. F. Torrance. Grand Rapids, Mich.: Eerdmans, 1963.

Institutes of the Christian Religion. Edited by John T. McNeill. Philadelphia: Westminster, 1970.

The Cynic Epistles (English): *The Cynic Epistles: A Study Edition*. Edited and translated by Abraham J. Malherbe. SBLSBS 12. Missoula, Mont.: Scholars Press, 1979.

Didache. Two sources used:

(English and Greek): *The Didache: Text, Translation, Analysis, and Commentary*. Aaron Milavec, translator and author. Collegeville, Minn.: Liturgical Press, 2003.

(English): *Early Christian Writings: The Apostolic Fathers*. Translated by Maxwell Staniforth. Revised by Andrew Louth. London: Penguin, 1987.

Euripides (English): *Ten Plays by Euripides.* Translated by Moses Hadas and John McLean. New York: Bantam Books, 1960.

Greek New Testament: *Novum Testamentum Graece.* Nestle-Aland. Edited by Barbara and Kurt Aland, Johannes Karavidopoulos, Carlo M. Martini, and Bruce M. Metzger. Stuttgart: Deutsche Bibelgesellschaft, 1993.

Gregory of Nyssa: *The Later Christian Fathers: A Selection from the Writings of the Fathers from St. Cyril of Jerusalem to St. Leo the Great.* Edited by Henry Bettenson. Oxford: Oxford University Press, 1970.

Gregory the Great (English and Latin): *Gregory the Great: His Place in History and Thought, vol. II.* F. Homes Dudden, author. New York: Longmans, Green & Co., 1905.

Hebrew Bible: *Biblia Hebraica Stuttgartensia.* Edited by K. Elliger and W. Rudolph. Stuttgart: Württembergische Bibelanstalt Stuttgart, 1976.

Irenaeus (English and Greek): *The Idea of the Atonement in Christian Theology.* Hastings Rashdall. London: Macmillan, 1919.

Luther, Martin. Three English sources used:

   A Commentary on St. Paul's Epistle to the Galatians. Revised translation based on the Middleton English edition. London: Clarke & Co., 1953.

   Martin Luther: Selections from His Writings. Edited by John Dillenberger. Garden City, N.Y.: Doubleday, 1961.

   What Luther Says. Edited and Translated by Ewald M. Plass. St. Louis: Concordia Publishing House, 1959.

Philo (English): *The Works of Philo.* Translated by C. D. Yonge. Peabody, Mass.: Hendrickson, 1993.

Plato (English and Greek):

   Laws. Translated by Robert Gregg Bury, Loeb Classical Library, *Plato* vol. 10. London: Wm. Heinemann and New York: G. P. Putnam's Sons, 1926.

   Theaetatus. Translated by H. N. Fowler, Loeb Classical Library, *Plato* vol. 2. London: Wm. Heinemann and New York: G. P. Putnam's Sons, 1921.

Septuagint (Greek): *Septuaginta: Id est Vetus Testamentum Graece iuxta LXX interpres.* Edited by Alfred Rahlfs. Stuttgart: Deutsche Bibelgesellschaft, 1979 [1935].

Testaments of the Twelve Patriarchs (English): *The Old Testament Pseudepigrapha,* vol. 1. Edited by James H. Charlesworth. New York: Doubleday, 1983.

Secondary Sources:

Anderson, Gary. "The Interpretation of the Purification Offering חטאת[1] in the *Temple Scroll* (11QTemple) and Rabbinic Literature." *JBL* 111 (1992) 17–35.

———. "Sacrifice and Sacrificial Offerings (OT)." Pages 870–86 in *Anchor Bible Dictionary* V. New York: Doubleday, 1994.

Aulén, Gustaf. *Christus Victor: An Historical Study of the Three Main Types of the Idea of the Atonement.* London: Society for Promoting Christian Knowledge, 1931.

---

[1] [ḥaṭṭaʾt].

Bailey, Daniel P. "Concepts of *Stellvertretung* in the Interpretation of Isaiah 53." Pages 223–50 in *Jesus and the Suffering Servant: Isaiah 53 and Christian Origins*. Edited by William H. Bellinger Jr., and William R. Farmer. Harrisburg, Penn.: Trinity Press International, 1998.

———. "Jesus as the Mercy Seat: The Semantics and Theology of Paul's Use of *Hilastērion* in Romans 3:25." Ph.D. diss., Cambridge University, 1999.

Bartlett, Anthony W. *Cross Purposes: The Violent Grammar of Christian Atonement*. Harrisburg: Trinity, 2001.

Bauer, Walter. *A Greek-English Lexicon of the New Testament and Other Early Christian Literature*. Translated and adapted by William F. Arndt and F. Wilbur Gingrich. Second edition. Chicago: University of Chicago Press, 1979.

Baxter, Christina A. "The Cursed Beloved: A Reconsideration of Penal Substitution." Pages 54–72 in *Atonement Today*. Edited by John Goldingay. London: SPCK, 1995.

Bell, Daniel M., Jr. "Sacrifice and Suffering: Beyond Justice, Human Rights, and Capitalism." *Modern Theology* 18 (2002) 333–59.

Berdyaev, Nicolas. *Christianity and Anti-Semitism*. New York: Philosophical Library, 1954.

———. *Christian Existentialism*. Edited by Daniel Lowrie. New York: Harper & Row, 1965.

———. *The Divine and the Human*. London: Geoffrey Bles, 1949.

Boyarin, Daniel. *A Radical Jew: Paul and the Politics of Identity*. Berkeley: University of California Press, 1994.

Braaten, C. E. and R. W. Jensen, editors. *Union With Christ: The New Finnish Interpretation of Luther*. Grand Rapids, Mich.: Eerdmans, 1998.

Brown, Joanne Carlson and Rebecca Parker. "For God So Loved the World?" Pages 1–30 in *Christianity, Patriarchy, and Abuse: A Feminist Critique*. Edited by Joanne Carlson Brown and Carole R. Bohn. New York: Pilgrim, 1989.

Bruce, F. F. *This Is That: The New Testament Development of Some Old Testament Themes*. Exeter, U.K.: Paternoster Press, 1968.

Burkert, Walter. *Greek Religion: Archaic and Classical*. Translated by John Raffan. Oxford: Blackwell, 1985.

———. *Structure and History in Greek Mythology and Ritual*. Sather Classical Lectures 47.

Campbell, R. J. *Christianity and the Social Order*. London: Chapman and Hall, 1907.

Carson, D. A. "Atonement in Romans 3:21-26." Pages 119–39 in *The Glory of the Atonement: Biblical, Historical and Practical Perspectives*. Edited by Charles E. Hill and Frank A. James III. Downers Grove, Ill.: IVP, 2004.

Chilton, Bruce. *The Temple of Jesus: His Sacrificial Program within a Cultural History of Sacrifice*. University Park: Pennsylvania State University Press, 1992.

Ciholas, Paul. "Knowledge and Faith: Pauline Platonisms and the Spiritualization of Reality." *PRSt* 3 (1976) 188–201.

Crysdale, Cynthia S. W. *Embracing Travail: Retrieving the Cross Today*. New York: Continuum, 1999.

Daly, Robert J., s.j. *Christian Sacrifice: the Judaeo-Christian Background Before Origen.* Catholic University of America Studies in Christian Antiquity 18. Washington: The Catholic University of America Press, 1978.

Dennis, John. "The Function of the חטאת[2] Sacrifice in the Priestly Literature." *ETL* 78,1 (2002) 108–29.

deSilva, David A. *4 Maccabees.* Guides to Apocrypha and Pseudepigrapha. Sheffield: Sheffield Academic, 1998.

Dodd, C. H. *The Bible and the Greeks.* London: Hodder and Stoughton, 1935.

Douglas, Mary. "Justice as the Cornerstone: An Interpretation of Leviticus 18–20." *Interpretation* 53 (1999) 341–50.

———. *Natural Symbols: Explorations in Cosmology.* New York: Pantheon, 1982.

———. *Purity and Danger: An Analysis of Concepts of Pollution and Taboo.* New York: Frederick A. Praeger, 1966.

Dundes, Alan. "The Ritual Murder or Blood Libel Legend: A Study of Anti-Semitic Victimization through Projective Inversion." Pages 336–76 in *The Blood Libel Legend: A Casebook in Anti-Semitic Folklore.* Madison: University of Wisconsin Press, 1989.

Dunn, James D. G. *Jesus, Paul, and the Law: Studies in Mark and Galatians.* Louisville, Ky.: Westminster, 1990.

———. "Paul's Understanding of the Death of Jesus." Pages 35–56 in *Sacrifice and Redemption: Durham Essays in Theology.* Edited by S. W. Sykes. Cambridge: Cambridge University Press, 1991.

———. *Romans 1–8.* Word Biblical Commentary 38A. Dallas: Word, 1988.

———. *The Theology of Paul the Apostle.* Grand Rapids, Mich.: Eerdmans, 1998.

Ehrman, Bart D. "The Cup, The Bread, and the Salvific Effect of Jesus' Death in Luke–Acts," Pages 576–91 in *SBLSP* 1991. Edited by Eugene H. Lovering Jr. Atlanta: Scholars Press, 1991.

Elliott, Susan Margaret. "The Rhetorical Strategy of Paul's Letter to the Galatians in Its Anatolian Cultic Context: Circumcision and the Castration of the *Galli* of the Mother of the Gods." Ph.D. dissertation, Loyola University Chicago, 1997.

Engberg-Pedersen, Troels. *Paul and the Stoics.* Louisville, Ky.: Westminster John Knox, 2000.

Evans, Christopher F. *Saint Luke.* London: SCM, 1990.

Ferguson, Everett. "Spiritual Sacrifice in Early Christianity and Its Environ-ment." *ANRW* 23.2:1151–89. Part 2, *Principat* 23.2. Edited by W. Haase. New York: de Gruyter, 1980.

Fitzmyer, Joseph A. *The Gospel According to Luke (X–XXIV).* Anchor Bible 28A. Garden City, N.Y.: Doubleday, 1985.

Fitzpatrick, P. J. "On Eucharistic Sacrifice in the Middle Ages." Pages 129–56 in *Sacrifice and Redemption: Durham Essays in Theology.* Edited by S. W. Sykes. Cambridge: Cambridge University Press, 1991.

---

[2] [*ḥaṭṭaʾt*].

Foley, Helene P. *Ritual Irony: Poetry and Sacrifice in Euripides.* Ithaca, N.Y.: Cornell University Press, 1985.

Fudge, Edward William and Robert A. Peterson. *Two Views of Hell: A Biblical and Theological Dialogue.* Downers Grove, Ill.: IVP, 2000.

Gaster, T. H. "Sacrifices and Offerings, OT." Pages 147–59 in vol. 4 of *The Interpreter's Dictionary of the Bible.* Edited by George Arthur Buttrick. 4 vols. New York: Abingdon, 1962.

Gese, Hartmut. *Essays on Biblical Theology.* Minneapolis: Augsburg, 1981.

Gibson, Jeffrey. "Paul's 'Dying Formula': Prolegomena to an Understanding of Its Import and Significance." Paper presented at the Annual Meeting of the SBL. Toronto, Ontario, November 25, 2002. 22 pages.

Girard, René. *I See Satan Fall Like Lightning.* Translated by James G. Williams. Maryknoll, New York: Orbis, 2001.

———. *Things Hidden Since the Foundation of the World.* London: Athlone, 1987.

———. "Violence, Difference, Sacrifice: A Conversation with René Girard." Interviewed by Rebecca Adams. *Religion and Literature* 25.2 (1993) 9–33.

Goldingay, John. "Old Testament Sacrifice and the Death of Christ." Pages 3–20 in *Atonement Today.* Edited by John Goldingay. London: SPCK, 1995.

Gorman, Frank H., Jr. *The Ideology of Ritual: Space, Time and Status in the Priestly Theology.* JSOT Sup 91. Sheffield: Sheffield Academic, 1990.

Gorringe, Timothy. *God's Just Vengeance: Crime, Violence and the Rhetoric of Salvation.* Cambridge Studies in Ideology and Religion 9. Cambridge: Cambridge University Press, 1996.

Grabbe, Lester L. "The Scapegoat Tradition: A Study in Early Jewish Interpretation." *JSJ* 18 (1987) 152–67.

Green, Joel B. and Mark D. Baker. *Recovering the Scandal of the Cross: Atonement in New Testament and Contemporary Contexts.* Downers Grove, Ill.: IVP, 2000.

Gunther, John J. *St. Paul's Opponents and Their Background: A Study of Apocalyptic and Jewish Sectarian Teachings.* NovTSup 35. Leiden: E. J. Brill, 1973.

Gunton, Colin E. *The Actuality of Atonement: A Study of Metaphor, Rationality and the Christian Tradition.* Grand Rapids, Mich.: Eerdmans, 1989.

Hamerton-Kelly, Robert G. "Sacred Violence and Sinful Desire: Paul's Interpretation of Adam's Sin." Pages 35–54 in *The Conversation Continues: Studies in Paul and John in Honor of J. Louis Martyn.* Edited by Robert T. Fortna and Beverly R. Gaventa. Nashville: Abingdon, 1990.

———. *Sacred Violence: Paul's Hermeneutic of the Cross.* Minneapolis: Augsburg Fortress, 1992.

Harnack, Adolf von. *History of Dogma,* in 7 volumes. Translated by Neil Buchanan. New York: Dover, 1961 (1900).

Harris, Rendel. *The Glory of the Atonement.* London: Headley Brothers, 1915.

Harrison, Jane Ellen. *Prolegomena to the Study of Greek Religion.* Cambridge: Cambridge University Press, 1903.

Hartley, John E. *Leviticus.* WBC 4. Dallas: Word Books, 1992.

Hayward, C.T.R. *The Jewish Temple: A Non-biblical Sourcebook.* London: Routledge, 1996.

Hays, John H. "Atonement in the Book of Leviticus." *Interpretation* 52 (1998) 5–15.

Heim, S. Mark. "Christ Crucified." Pages 12–7 in *Christian Century* 118 no. 8 (March 7, 2001).

Hengel, Martin. *The Atonement: The Origins of the Doctrine in the New Testament.* London: SCM, 1981.

Hill, David. *Greek Words and Hebrew Meanings: Studies in the Semantics of Soteriological Terms.* Cambridge: Cambridge University Press, 1967.

Hofius, Otfried. "The Fourth Servant Song in the New Testament Letters." Pages 163–88 in *The Suffering Servant Song in the Jewish and Christian Sources.* Edited by Bernd Janowski and Peter Stuhlmacher. Translated by Daniel P. Bailey. Grand Rapids, Mich.: Eerdmans, 2004.

———. *Paulusstudien.* WUNT 51. Tübingen: J.C.B. Mohr, 1989.

Holten, Wilko van. "Can the Traditional View of Hell Be Defended? An Evaluation of Some Arguments for Eternal Punishment." *ATR* 85 (2003) 457–76.

Hooker, Morna D. "Interchange in Christ." *JTS* n.s. 22 (1971) 349–61.

———. *Not Ashamed of the Gospel: New Testament Interpretations of the Death of Christ.* Grand Rapids, Mich.: Eerdmans, 1994.

Hughes, Dennis D. *Human Sacrifice in Ancient Greece.* London: Routledge, 1991.

Janowski, Bernd. *Sühne als Heilsgeschehen: Studien zur Sühnetheologie der Priesterschrift und zur Wurzel KPR im Alten Orient und im Alten Testament.* WMANT 55. Düsseldorf: Neukirchener Verlag, 1982.

Judisch, Douglas McC. L. "Propitiation in the Language and Typology of the OT." *CTQ* 48 (1984) 221–43.

Kelly, J.N.D. *Early Christian Doctrines.* Revised edition. New York: Harper & Row, 1978.

Kiuchi, N. *The Purification Offering in the Priestly Literature: Its Meaning and Function.* JSOT Sup 56. Sheffield: Sheffield Academic, 1987.

Knohl, Israel. "The Sin Offering Law in the 'Holiness School.'" Pages 192–203 in *Priesthood and Cult in Ancient Israel.* Edited by Gary A. Anderson and Saul M. Olyan. JSOT Sup 125. Sheffield: Sheffield Academic, 1991.

Koch, Klaus. "The Translation of *kapporet* in the Septuagint." Pages 65–75 in *Pomegranates and Golden Bells: Studies in Biblical, Jewish, and Near Eastern Ritual, Law, and Literature in Honor of Jacob Milgrom.* Edited by David P. Wright, David Noel Freedman, and Avi Hurvitz. Winona Lake, Ind.: Eisenbrauns, 1995.

Kraus, Wolfgang. *Der Tod Jesu als Heiligtumsweihe: Eine Untersuchung zum Umfeld der Sühnevorstellung in Römer 3,25–26a.* WMANT 66. Düsseldorf: Neukirchener Verlag, 1991.

Lake, Kirsopp. *The Earlier Epistles of St. Paul: Their Motive and Origin.* Second edition. London: Rivingtons, 1919.

Lamont, Daniel. *The Creative Work of Jesus.* London: James Clarke & Co., 1924.

Levenson, Jon D. *The Death and Resurrection of the Beloved Son: The Transformation of Child Sacrifice in Judaism and Christianity.* New Haven, Conn.: Yale University Press, 1993.

Levine, Baruch A. *Leviticus: The Traditional Hebrew Text with the New JPS Translation*. The JPS Torah Commentary. Philadelphia: Jewish Publication Society, 1989.

Lyonnet, Stanislas. "The Terminology of Redemption." Pages 61–184 in *Sin, Redemption and Sacrifice: A Biblical and Patristic Study*, by Stanislas Lyonnet and Léopold Sabourin. Analecta Biblica 48. Rome: Biblical Institute, 1970.

Malherbe, Abraham J. *Paul and the Popular Philosophers*. Minneapolis: Fortress, 1989.

———. *Paul and the Thessalonians: The Philosophic Tradition of Pastoral Care*. Philadelphia: Fortress, 1989.

Mannermaa, Tuomo. "Why Is Luther So Fascinating? Modern Finnish Luther Research." Pages 1–20 in *Union With Christ: The New Finnish Interpretation of Luther*. Grand Rapids, Mich.: Eerdmans, 1998.

Martin, Dale. *Slavery as Salvation: The Metaphor of Slavery in Pauline Christianity*. New Haven, Conn.: Yale University Press, 1990.

McGuckin, J. A. "Sacrifice and Atonement: An Investigation into the Attitude of Jesus of Nazareth towards Cultic Sacrifice." Pages 648–61 in *Remembering for the Future: Working Papers and Addenda; Volume 1: Jews and Christians During and After the Holocaust*. Edited by Yehuda Bauer and others. Oxford: Pergamon, 1989.

McIntyre, John. Review of Michael Winter, *The Atonement*. *SJOT* 49 (1996) 123–4.

McKane, William. "Prophet and Institution." *ZAW* 94 (1982) 251–66.

McKelvey, R. J. *The New Temple: The Church in the New Testament*. Oxford Theological Monographs. Oxford: Oxford University Press, 1969.

McLean, Bradley Hudson. *The Cursed Christ: Mediterranean Expulsion Rituals and Pauline Soteriology*. JSNT Sup 126. Sheffield: Sheffield Academic, 1996.

Merkel, H. Καταλλάσσω, κτλ.[3] Pages 261–3 in *Exegetical Dictionary of the New Testament*, volume 2. Edited by Horst Balz and Gerhard Schneider. Grand Rapids, Mich.: Eerdmans, 1991.

Milavec, Aaron. *The Didache: Text, Translation, Analysis, and Commentary*. Collegeville, Minn.: Liturgical Press, 2003.

Milgrom, Jacob. "Further on the Expiatory Sacrifices." *JBL* 115 (1996) 511–4.

———. "Kipper." Pages 1039–44 in *Encyclopaedia Judaica*, volume 10. New York: The Macmillan Company, 1971.

———. *Leviticus*, 3 volumes: *Leviticus 1–16* (AB 3); *17–22* (AB 3A); *23–27* (AB 3B). Garden City, N.Y.: Doubleday, 1991, 2000, 2001.

———. "The Priestly Laws of Sancta Contamination." *"Sha'arei Talmon": Studies in the Bible, Qumran, and the Ancient Near East Presented to Shemaryahu Talmon."* Edited by Michael Fishbane and Emanuel Tov, 137–46. Winona Lake, Ind.: Eisenbrauns, 1992.

———. *Studies in Cultic Theology and Terminology*. SJLA 36. Leiden: E. J. Brill, 1983.

Moo, Douglas J. *The Epistle to the Romans*. Grand Rapids, Mich.: Eerdmans, 1996.

Morland, Kjell Arne. *The Rhetoric of Curse in Galatians: Paul Confronts Another Gospel*. Emory Studies in Early Christianity. Scholars Press, 1995.

[3] *[Katallassō, ktl]*.

Morris, Leon. *The Apostolic Preaching of the Cross.* Third edition, revised. Grand Rapids, Mich.: Eerdmans, 1965.

Moule, C.F.D. "Preaching the Atonement." *Epworth Review* 10, no. 2 (1983) 70–8.

Nelson-Pallmeyer, Jack. *Jesus Against Christianity: Reclaiming the Missing Jesus.* Harrisburg, Penn.: Trinity, 2001.

Nessan, Craig L. "Violence and Atonement." *Dialog* 35 (1996) 26–34.

Niebuhr, H. Richard. *Christ and Culture.* New York: Harper & Row, 1951.

Pardee, Nancy. "The Curse That Saves (*Didache* 16.5)." Pages 156–76 in *The Didache in Context: Essays on Its Text, History and Transmission.* Edited by Clayton N. Jefford. NovTSup 77. Leiden: E. J. Brill, 1995.

Parker, Robert. *Miasma: Pollution and Purification in Early Greek Religion.* Oxford: Clarendon, 1983.

Peters, Ted. "Atonement and the Final Scapegoat." *PRSt* 19 (1992) 151–81.

———. "Sin, Scapegoating, and Justifying Faith." *Dialog* 39 (2000) 84–92.

Phillips, J. B. *The Gospels Translated into Modern English.* New York: Macmillan, 1961.

Puchniak, Robert. "Augustine's Conception of Deification Revisited." To be published in *Theōsis: Deification in Christian Theology.* Edited by Stephen Finlan and Vladimir Kharlamov (Eugene, Ore.: Wipf & Stock, 2005).

Rashdall, Hastings. *The Idea of the Atonement in Christian Theology.* London: Macmillan, 1919.

Reumann, John. "The Gospel of the Righteousness of God: Pauline Interpretation in Romans 3:21-31." *Interpretation* 20 (1966) 432–52.

Riches, John. *Jesus and the Transformation of Judaism.* New York: Seabury, 1980.

Robertson, Archibald. *A Critical and Exegetical Commentary on the First Epistle of St. Paul to the Corinthians.* ICC. Edinburgh: T & T Clark, 1911.

Roetzel, Calvin J. *Paul: The Man and the Myth.* Edinburgh: T & T Clark, 1999.

Sanders, E. P. *Paul and Palestinian Judaism.* Philadelphia: Fortress, 1977.

Sansom, M. C. "Laying on of Hands in the Old Testament." *ExpT* 94 (1982–3) 323–6.

Schenker, Adrian. *Versöhnung und Sühne: Wege gewaltfreier Konfliktlösung im Alten Testament mit einem Ausblick auf das Neue Testament.* Biblische Beiträge 15. Freiberg: Verlag Schweizerisches Katholisches Bibelwerk, 1981.

Schoeps, Hans-Joachim. "Ebionite Christianity." *JTS* n.s. 4 (1953) 219–24.

Schwartz, Baruch J. "The Prohibitions Concerning the 'Eating' of Blood in Leviticus 17." Pages 34–66 in *Priesthood and Cult in Ancient Israel.* Edited by Gary A. Anderson and Saul M. Olyan. JSOT Sup 125. Sheffield: Sheffield Academic, 1991.

Sherman, Robert. *King, Priest, and Prophet: A Trinitarian Theology of Atonement.* New York: T & T Clark, 2004.

Smith, Brian K. and Wendy Doniger. "Sacrifice and Substitution: Ritual Mystification and Mythical Demystification." *Numen* 36 (1989) 189–224.

Soloviev, Vladimir (but here spelled Vladimir Solovyev). *God, Man and the Church: The Spiritual Foundations of Life*. Translated by Donald Attwater. London: James Clarke, 1938.

————. *Lectures on Divine Humanity*. Hudson, New York: Lindisfarne, 1995.

Stählin, Gustav. "περίψημα"[4] Pages 84–93 in *TDNT* 6. Grand Rapids, Mich.: Eerdmans, 1968.

Stökl Ben Ezra, Daniel. *The Impact of Yom Kippur on Early Christianity: The Day of Atonement from Second Temple Judaism to the Fifth Century*. WUNT 163. Tübingen: J.C.B. Mohr, 2003.

Stowers, Stanley K. *A Rereading of Romans: Justice, Jews, and Gentiles*. New Haven, Conn.: Yale University Press, 1994.

Stuhlmacher, Peter. *Reconciliation, Law and Righteousness: Essays in Biblical Theology*. Philadelphia: Fortress, 1986.

Thayer, Joseph Henry. Translator and enlarger. From Grimm. *A Greek-English Lexicon of the New Testament*, Fourth edition. Edinburgh: T & T Clark, 1901.

Thompson, James W. "Hebrews 9 and Hellenistic Concepts of Sacrifice." *JBL* 98 (1979): 567–78.

Tomson, Peter J. *Paul and the Jewish Law: Halakha in the Letters of the Apostle to the Gentiles*. Minneapolis: Fortress Press, 1990.

Van Henten, Jan Willem and Friedrich Avemarie, editors. *Martyrdom and Noble Death: Selected Texts from Graeco-Roman, Jewish and Christian Antiquity*. London: Routledge, 2002.

Van Henten, Jan Willem. *The Maccabean Martyrs as Saviours of the Jewish People: A Study of 2 and 4 Maccabees*. JSJ Sup 57. Leiden: Brill, 1997.

————. "The Tradition-Historical Background of Rom 3:25: A Search for Pagan and Jewish Parallels." Pages 101–28 in *From Jesus to John: Essays on Jesus and New Testament Christology in Honour of Marinus de Jonge*. Edited by Martinus C. De Boer. JSNT Sup 84. Sheffield: JSOT Press, 1993.

Versnel, H. S. "Self-Sacrifice, Compensation, and the Anonymous Gods." Pages 135–94 in *Le Sacrifice dans l'Antiquité*. Geneva: Vandoeuvres, 1980.

Watson, Frances. *Paul, Judaism and the Gentiles: A Sociological Approach*. Cambridge: Cambridge University Press, 1986.

Weaver, J. Denny. *The Nonviolent Atonement*. Grand Rapids, Mich.: Eerdmans, 2001.

————. "Violence in Christian Theology." *Cross Currents* 51 (2001) 150–76.

Westermann, Claus. *Isaiah 40–66*. London: SCM, 1969.

Wheeler, David L. "The Cross and the Blood: Dead or Living Images?" *Dialog* 35 (1996) 7–13.

Williams, James G. *The Bible, Violence, and the Sacred: Liberation from the Myth of Sanctioned Violence*. San Francisco: Harper San Francisco, 1991.

---

[4] *[peripsēma].*

————. "Steadfast Love and Not Sacrifice." Pages 71–99 in *Curing Violence*. Edited by Mark I. Wallace and Theophilus H. Smith. Forum Facsimiles 3. Sonoma, Calif.: Polebridge Press, 1994.

Williams Sam K. *Jesus' Death as Saving Event: The Background and Origin of a Concept*. HDR 2. Missoula, Mont.: Scholars Press, 1975.

Willi-Plein, Ina. *Opfer und Kult im alttestamentlichen Israel: Textbefragungen und Zwischenrgebnisse*. Stuttgart: Verlag Katholisches Bibelwerk, 1993.

Wink, Walter. *Engaging the Powers: Discernment and Resistance in a World of Domination*. Minneapolis: Fortress, 1992.

————. *The Powers That Be: Theology for a New Millennium*. New York: Doubleday, 1998.

Winter, Michael. *The Atonement*. Problems in Theology. Collegeville, Minn.: Liturgical Press, 1995.

Workman, George Coulson. *At Onement: Or, Reconciliation with God*. New York: Fleming H. Revell, 1911.

Wright, David P. "Day of Atonement." Pages 70–6 in *ABD* II. New York: Doubleday, 1987.

————. *The Disposal of Impurity: Elimination Rites in the Bible and in Hittite and Mesopotamian Literature*. SBLDS 101. Atlanta: Scholars, 1987.

Wright, N. T. *The Climax of the Covenant: Christ and the Law in Pauline Theology*. Edinburgh: T & T Clark, 1991.

————. *Jesus and the Victory of God*. Volume 2 of *Christian Origins and the Question of God*. Minneapolis: Fortress, 1996.

————. *The Resurrection of the Son of God*. Volume 3 of *Christian Origins and the Question of God*. Minneapolis: Fortress, 2003.

Yerkes, Royden Keith. *Sacrifice in Greek and Roman Religions and Early Judaism*. London: Adam and Charles Black, 1953.

Young, Frances M. *Sacrifice and the Death of Christ*. Cambridge: Cambridge University Press, 1975.

————. "Temple Cult and Law in Early Christianity: A Study in the Relationship between Jews and Christians in the Early Centuries." *NTS* 19 (1972–3) 325–8.

Index of Modern Authors

Index of Ancient Texts